CREATIVE DECORATIONS
WITH DRIED FLOWERS

Drawings by Marion Seiler
Photographs by William Brinkhous
except where noted

Creative Decorations With Dried Flowers

Dorothea Schnibben Thompson

HEARTHSIDE PRESS INCORPORATED

Publishers • New York

DEDICATION

To my husband and children
My grateful thanks for their love,
understanding and patience.

ACKNOWLEDGEMENT

Sincere thanks to my many friends who have let me wander through their gardens and pick the cream of their floral crop for drying. Their beautiful flowers enhance the arrangements and decorations throughout this book.

To my friends, Addie Totten and Cherry Parker, I give special thanks for their continued interest and encouragement.

CONTENTS

INTRODUCTION

The art of drying flowers is not new. As early as the eighteenth century dried flowers were used for winter bouquets. Flowers were hung in the attic or barn loft to dry; weeds were dipped in homemade dyes for a touch of color. Later on came the burying method, using borax, corn meal or sand. Today, a thirsty chemical known as silica gel is widely used to preserve flowers faster and better than ever. That "last rose of summer" from a friend's formal garden, a child's fistful of field daisies, a greenhouse orchid, a bunch of pansies from a street vendor's cart—these need no longer be a soon-wilted bouquet or a fleeting memory. Instead, they can add color and charm to your home, as permanent keepsakes and glamorous accessories.

The idea of developing a medium for drying flowers for more natural color and form was sparked when I was asked to make some dried arrangements for a church bazaar. Someone had dried by the "hanging" method a vast amount of material which I was to use in making the arrangements. There were many color limitations by this method of drying and I soon discovered I was not satisfied with the grass tones, or the browns, greys and yellows. Also, I did not like the shriveled look of the flowers. I determined to see if the natural form of the flowers, plus their beautiful color, could be preserved. My husband, a professional engineer with a deep interest in chemistry, suggested silica gel. Silica gel has long been used in industrial laboratories to absorb moisture and is used for the same purpose closer to home—in small packets in packages of potato chips and cereals.

My first experiment with silica gel was in drying a purple orchid left from Easter. Its perfect form and color were astounding! This was all the encouragement I needed—I started drying everything in sight and, after experimenting for several years with excellent results, introduced my technique of drying with silica gel to the public in the August 1961 issue of *American Home*. Subsequently the late Mr. Theodore A. Weston, then Garden Editor, wrote me:

"I'm sure your article has stirred up more interest than any garden or flower arrangement story we've run in recent years. We've been literally swamped with inquiries, almost half of them from druggists, and so there is no telling how many people have been motivated by the article either directly or indirectly.

"The Davison Chemical Company of Baltimore, which is a division of W. R. Grace & Company, is the primary source of the material and, therefore, became involved in the supply problem as soon as the August issue reached our readers. Their advertising representative phoned me when the inquiries began to mount up to get some idea of how many people in the country might be possible purchasers of silica gel for drying flowers. When I told him the total might be close to five million the firm evidently decided to make a real crash program of getting into production with it. By August 2 they were actually making deliveries of their ready-to-use silica gel preparation under the name of Flower-Dri! The Plantabbs Corporation, also of Baltimore, was given the exclusive distribution of the product and ever since has been hard pressed to keep up with the rapidly expanding demand. They expect to have Flower-Dri distributed nationally in all stores where garden products are sold within a very few weeks.

"The American Home Promotion Department is intending to publicize the fact that this whole 'flower drying business' started with your article in the August *American Home*—just in case it might otherwise happen that the origin of Flower-Dri were lost sight of!"

In the subsequent years since I first developed the process, I have continued to work with silica gel and particularly with the dried material which resulted. Here, now in book form, I give for the first time my complete method of drying flowers and foliage, as well as ideas for using the preserved flowers in varied decorative ways.

CREATIVE DECORATIONS WITH DRIED FLOWERS

I The New Way of Preserving Plant Material

SILICA GEL, THE THIRSTY CHEMICAL

Silica gel is a chemical compound that looks and feels like ordinary table salt. It is actually not a "gel" at all. Made from sodium silicate and sulfuric acid, it forms a jelly-like mass called hydrogel during one state in the manufacturing process. The end product, however, is in the form of hard granules like sand. In different blends it has hundreds of varied applications, from acting as a catalyst for cracking petroleum, to absorbing the moisture in packaged cereals, potato chips and baby powders. When used as a dehydrating agent, silica gel can take on up to forty per cent of its weight in water vapor—be soaking wet in fact, yet look and feel as dry as dust.

Silica gel, readily available, is packaged especially for drying flowers under the trade name of Flower-Dri (see Sources of Supply). It may be purchased from department, seed and hardware stores, garden supply centers, florists, and by mail order. And, remember, your initial cost is your only cost because silica gel is used over and over again. It never wears out!

RE-USING SILICA GEL

Silica gel, packaged for drying flowers, is a mixture of two mesh sizes. The white is as fine as table salt, the blue Tel-Tale crystals are of a coarser mesh. The blue crystals, by turning pink, tell you when the chemical has absorbed its maximum amount of water and needs to be dried for re-use. To remove the moisture, spread out the mixture in a large open pan and place it in a 250° F. oven for about thirty minutes. As soon as the crystals have turned blue, the silica gel is re-activated. Pour it into an airtight container until you are ready to use it. Silica gel must be kept airtight or it will absorb moisture from the air.

Since some flowers contain more water than others, the mixture might need the oven treatment after one use. With other flowers, it may be used several times. As long as you see some blue crystals, you may continue to use it. The oven treatment is needed only when the Tel-Tale blue crystals have turned pink. Step-by-step directions for using silica gel follow.

CONTAINERS FOR DRYING

Any container with a tight-fitting cover may be used for the drying process. I use fruitcake tins in several sizes and coffee tins. I do not recommend a flexible plastic container because the sides bend away from the lids and let in air. A rigid plastic container with a sealable lid would be satisfactory. The new plastic shoe boxes are exceptionally good for spikes of larkspur, snapdragon and dusty miller. Also, the large fruitcake tins will take care of large leaves and sprays of flowers. Coffee tins are good for miniature flowers and for one large flower. Remember, however, to seal the cover in place with freezer or masking tape. Any cover that fits tightly will not need further taping. The main object is, of course, to keep out any moisture in the air during the drying process.

GENERAL DIRECTIONS FOR DRYING

Pour silica gel into a sealable container to a depth of about one and one-half inches. Insert short-stemmed flowers *face up*. Space them so they are not touching. Plate 1. (Note: To economize on silica gel, crush aluminum foil to a depth of one and one-half inches in bottom of container and, with an ice pick, make holes at intervals to hold stems.)

Slowly sprinkle silica gel over flowers until completely covered, gently working it up and around them so contact is made on all parts of the flowers. Plate 2.

Cover cake tin or other container with tight top and seal it with freezer or masking tape. Plate 3. Put it away in a dry place where the contents will not be disturbed for the period required for drying. (See Timing Period, page 24.)

To remove flowers, pour off mixture slowly until they are uncovered. Plate 4. Lift out gently and blow away any particles that adhere. Completely remove silica gel with a soft artist's brush. The chemical will brush off easily.

Store flowers away from light in a sealed, airtight container to which has been added about three tablespoons of blued silica gel. Plate 5. This storing will keep the flowers dry even during warm,

1.   Space flowers so they are not touching.

II.   Slowly sprinkle silica gel over flowers until completely covered.

humid weather. Widemouthed pint, quart and half-gallon Mason preserving jars are excellent for this purpose. Use the half-pint jars for a single flower and miniature blooms. Place the jars in packing cartons and stack them to save space.

DRYING BUDS AND FOLIAGE

All foliage, rose buds or any flower bud about one-fourth open should be laid horizontally in the container on about one-half inch of silica gel. Completely cover. Place blooms about half open at a 45-degree angle to avoid crushing the petals. Plate 6. By placing buds and foliage on the bottom, you can utilize your silica gel until you have reached a depth of about one and one-half inches. Then insert some flowers face up to fill your container. Of course, if you want to dry only buds and foliage, place layer over layer, covering each as you progress, until you reach the top.

SPIKES   Nothing dries more beautifully than larkspur and delphinium. Use the side shoots of delphinium and select blossoms which have a few green, unopened buds at the top. In drying these spikes, place them horizontally in the container and gently sprinkle silica gel around the sides first, gradually covering from the top. Remove the larger florets from the stalks of delphinium and dry them face up as individual flowers. Later you may add wire for a longer stem.

CARNATIONS   The directions apply to all flowers with one exception —the carnation. Before drying carnations, twist a pipe cleaner tightly around the base of the petals as shown in Figure 1-A. This will hold the petals close together and take care of the shrinkage during the drying process. Proceed to cover the flower completely as shown in the general directions.

III.   Seal tin with tape.

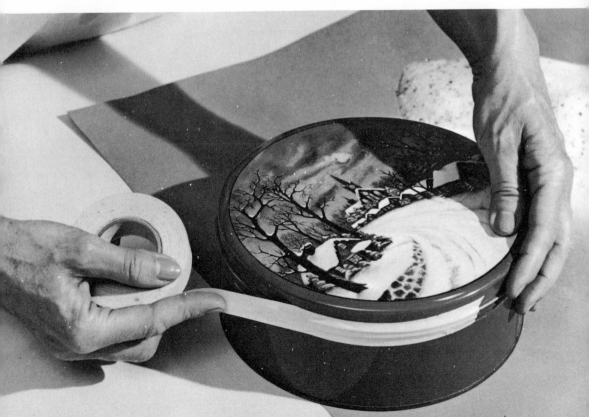

IV.   Gently pour off silica gel.

TIMING PERIOD

The time required for drying varies with the size, texture and moisture content of the flowers and foliage. However, any material will
dry within four to seven days. To be safe, allow seven days. You will
find that small flowers such as pansies, forget-me-nots and field daisies
will dry in less than four days. Hydrangea, ageratum and candytuft
will also dry very quickly. Flowers with many petals such as marigolds, carnations, dahlias, zinnias, and large roses and buds may
require up to a week, as will some foliage. Dusty miller, rose foliage
and many ferns will dry in just a few days, while English laurel,
elaeagnus, ivy and various berries will require the full seven days.
Always be on the safe side—let your materials stay in the silica gel
long enough to thoroughly dry. When drying, remember to pack to-

gether those flowers requiring less time to dry and, likewise, pack the larger, heavier flowers with many petals requiring more time in another container. By doing this, you will not tie up the use of your chemical. You can dry *two* cans of forget-me-nots, pansies, ageratum in one week, whereas the large roses, marigolds and dahlias will require about seven days to dry.

MAKING STEMS FOR FLOWERS AND FOLIAGE

Natural-looking stems for both flowers and foliage are made of wire and covered with floral tape. Individual wire stems afford more flexibility in creating your design—you can bend them to make a curve, fill a void, or hide the mechanics of your arrangement.

To make the stems for flowers and foliage, place a piece of No. 20 florist wire of the desired length next to the stem and join them together with a small piece of freezer or masking tape. This will hold

V.   *Store dried flowers in sealed containers.*

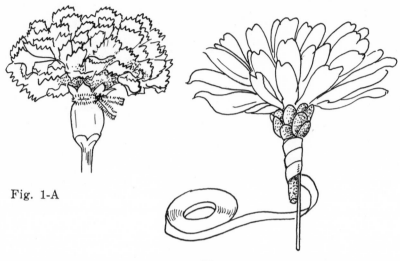

Fig. 1-A

Fig. 1-B

them securely. Then spiral wrap the stem with floral tape as far down as necessary. Figure 1-B. If the stem does not show in the arrangement, you need not cover it with floral tape. When the stem of a leaf is very short, attach a piece of wire to the back with Scotch tape and then spiral wrap the stem. Figure 1-C.

Remember, when all the moisture has been removed from flowers and foliage in the drying process, they are brittle, so handle them carefully. But don't be discouraged if a petal falls—simply apply a dab of Elmer's or Sobo glue and replace it. Flowers without stems can be used in making pictures and other decorations. Experience will soon show how much handling dried materials can endure.

Full-blown roses are likely to fall apart when dried. Therefore, dry them as buds to three-fourths open. Before drying the latter, I suggest that you cut the sepals close to the receptacle because when dried they will curl under and hinder you from attaching a wire stem. Figure 1-D. To strengthen a dried rose, apply a few drops of adhesive (Elmer's or Sobo) to the bottom where the petals are attached to the receptacle. With a toothpick, spread the glue thinly and allow it to dry before attempting to remove any adhering silica gel. The same strengthening procedure may be used on any flower if the petals appear loose and ready to fall.

PRESERVING DRIED FLOWERS WITH SPRAY AND WAX

I have found that a spraying of clear plastic makes dried flowers to be used as decoration far more durable, preserves their color and renders them moisture-resistant. I use Seymour's Clear Plastic Spray #11-821. For flowers especially affected by humidity, a dipping in melted paraffin, comfortable to touch, is good protection. With this coating, the materials are less brittle. Please note an exception: because of the weight of melted paraffin, a flower with a single row of petals, such as a cosmos, should not be dipped. Instead, use an empty tissue box, punch holes with an icepick and insert the short stems of the flowers. The surface of the box will support the petals. With a flat toothpick, gently paint on an even coat of melted paraffin and allow it to dry.

EQUIPMENT AND MATERIALS

Most of the items listed below are used in flower arranging and in making decorative items—perhaps you already have them. They are

Fig. 1-C

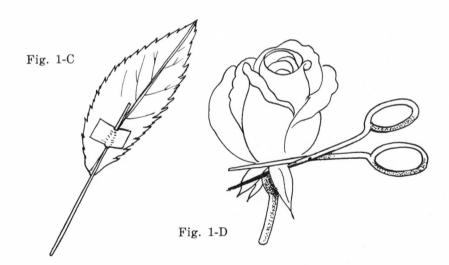

Fig. 1-D

inexpensive and can be purchased from florists, garden centers, department and hardware stores, etc. Also see Sources of Supply, page 121.

1. Tacky tape (I prefer it to floral clay for anchoring pinholders).
2. Several lightweight pinpoint holders, one-inch and two-inches.
3. Block of Oasis. Dry Oasis will be used in your containers instead of sand or styrofoam. It is much easier to insert stems in Oasis.
4. Florist's wire, sizes Nos. 18 and 20, for making stems.
5. Floral pliers for clipping stems and wire.
6. Roll of floral tape (moss green) for wrapping wire stems.
7. Freezer or masking tape for attaching flower to wire stem; also Scotch tape to mend tears. When adhesive tape is specified in the directions, I prefer freezer or masking tape.
8. Artist's brush for dusting silica gel from preserved flowers.
9. Clear adhesive (Elmer's or Sobo) to replace petals, for picture-making, and other gluing applications.
10. Seymour's Clear Plastic Spray #11-821 for preserving all dried materials.
11. Net tufts, when referred to in making various items, are three-inch net squares, pinched in the center and tied with thread, or when necessary, attached to round toothpick halves with fine wire.

PRESSED FLOWERS

Unlike drying flowers and foliage in their natural three-dimensional form, as explained in the previous section, all materials when pressed are flat. Pressed flowers are lovely in pictures (see Plate 7) where glass will protect the materials, or to decorate greeting cards and note paper as explained on page 103.

The flowers must be fresh, bright in color and interesting in design. Choose those having single thicknesses so that each petal will show. Press them as soon as they are picked to preserve the natural beauty. Be sure the flowers are thoroughly dry before using them. Flowers such as daisies, pansies, anemones, wild roses and ferns lie flat and will not crush when pressed. Select some curved stems and press them separately, splitting the thick ones.

To press, assemble a flat board, several bricks or other heavy objects, silica gel, two pieces of blotting paper, cleansing tissue and a large plastic bag.

VI.   *Place buds and foliage horizontally on bottom, blooms three-fourths open at 45-degree angle, full-blown face up.*

Cover the flat board with blotting paper large enough to hold the materials. Sprinkle about two tablespoons of silica gel over the surface and cover with a double thickness of cleansing tissue. Arrange your plant material the way you want it to dry. Cover with another layer of tissue, sprinkle again with the same amount of silica gel and place the second piece of blotting paper on top. Slip the board into a plastic bag and close the top with a pipe cleaner tightly twisted. Distribute the weight of bricks evenly on top. The materials will dry in a week.

Many designs can be fashioned from pressed plant material. Here are a few suggestions: dolls, clowns and animals from colorful flower petals; a garden or woodland scene; a pattern for a tapestry or wallpaper; a design to resemble embroidery.

VII.   A colorful souvenir of summer—pressed flowers pretty as a picture!

II   Notes on Flowers and Foliage

RETAINING COLOR

One of the remarkable attributes of silica gel is that it enables you to dry many flowers to retain all their natural color, as vivid and fresh as when growing. However, some flowers change color or turn a trifle darker. This does not detract from their beauty. In fact, clashing colors frequently become harmonious when they lose chroma or intensity. I have found that light colors usually dry their natural color, and dark colors tend to turn still darker in the drying process.

WHITE   White flowers when dried are inclined to be more cream than white. However, daisies, candytuft, dogwood, lilac and snowball *(Viburnum tomentosum)* are excellent for drying and appear almost snow-white. Touches of white will accent and add interest to your arrangement.

BLUE   For "true-blue," nothing will be more fresh-looking and natural than forget-me-not, delphinium (or larkspur) and hydrangea. Blue is also the most lasting of the colors. Lavender asters, dahlias and foxgloves stay true to color and are long lasting.

YELLOW AND ORANGE   The clear bright yellow of jonquils, zinnias, and snapdragons is also captured in drying and will last for many months, gradually fading to a soft cream. The bright orange of the marigold and tithonia is a must for vivid color.

31

PINK   Light to medium pinks show very little change, but the darker shades of pink deepen to rose or a rich red. These darker shades are needed to give your arrangement depth and interest. Pastel pinks, blending into reds and on to deepest maroons, create a rich color harmony.

FADING   You must remember that all colors fade, some more quickly than others, but the fading is so gradual that you are hardly aware of it. The flowers as they fade seem to "age" and the colors become more subtle and blend together. Preserved flowers will lose their color very rapidly if exposed to direct sunlight or placed in a brightly lighted room.

TEXTURE   Since the texture of flowers varies, some will naturally dry better than others. Flowers such as tulips and daffodils have an almost transparent texture when dried; roses and zinnias have substance and the texture does not change appreciably. Of course, you must expect a certain amount of shrinkage to occur in the drying process because all the moisture has been removed. Flowers with a single row of petals, like coreopsis or cosmos, will show more shrinkage than flowers with many petals, like marigold and zinnia. Experience with drying flowers and foliage will help you appreciate the many variations in texture, color and form.

PICKING SEASONS

Start drying flowers in early spring with lilies-of-the-valley, hyacinths and daffodils. Then gather those of early summer: peonies, roses, blue and purple and pink hydrangeas, larkspurs, pansies, daisies, forget-me-nots and snapdragons. Don't forget the lovely delphiniums in the vivid shades of blue and purple, the lavender-pink foxgloves, small single and double dahlias, and the moss green heads of hydrangea. Zinnias and marigolds are perfect for drying and can be gathered all summer. Remember to pick the indispensable dusty miller and blue and white salvia in the early bud stage. This is your filler material and you will need a quantity of it. Early fall will contribute small chrysanthemums and late roses.

Foliage should be dried throughout the season, starting early with the slender, tapering lily-of-the-valley leaves. They, especially, retain a soft green color and can be used on the reverse side for a satin luster.

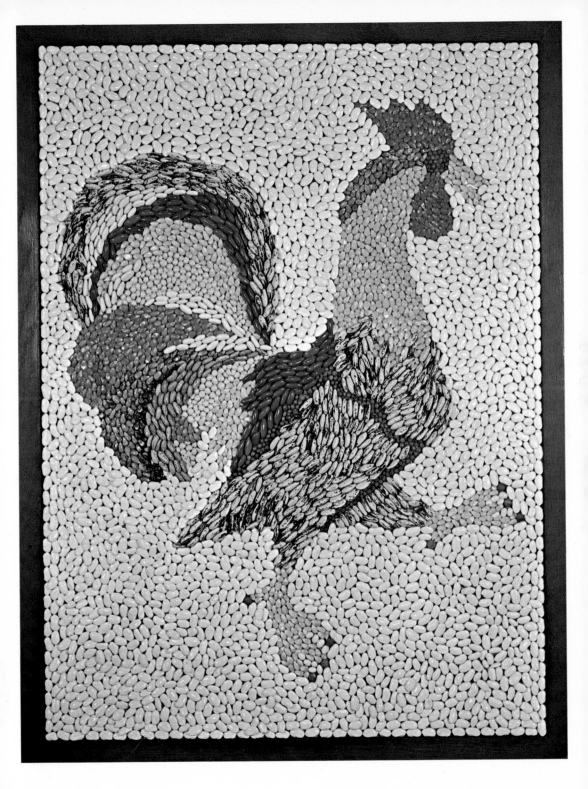

I.   *This rooster is made from chicken feed (what else?) following the pattern given on page 42.*

II.   Wear dried flowers for glamour. From left to right: a chignon bouquet, a hairpin from dried roses, a locket, an all-flower hat, earrings, brooch and a comb.

III. *(Below)* For a gala occasion, tiered brandy snifters, twelve, ten and eight inches high, are filled with flowers.

IV. *(Right)* Send a message on a handmade floral card. Tiny flowers, bits of velvet and touches of gold make them very special.

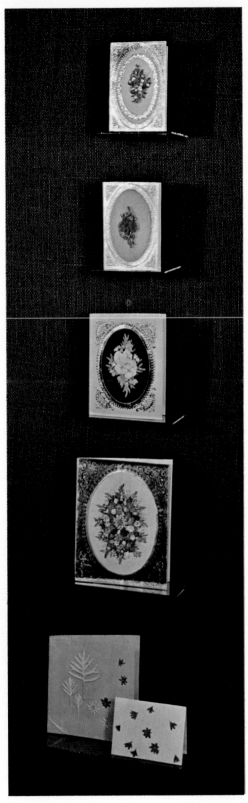

V.   *Roses from a formal garden and fern from a woodland path are arranged in an oval botany frame. Courtesy of The American Home Magazine.*

VI. *(Left)   Bright red celosia with laurel leaves are long lasting in a stark white china bowl.*

VII. *(Below)   Here comes the bride in satin and lace, carrying an old-fashioned fan bouquet (left) or colonial type (right).*

VIII. *(Below)* *A glass dome holds a colorful mass of flowers.*

IX. *(Opposite)* *Goblet of plenty—a review of summer's garden. Courtesy of The American Home Magazine.*

X. (Right) The antiqued arrangement is made of dried flowers and colored plastic flowers which have been dipped in gold paint.

XI. (Below) Dried floral decorations on gift wrappings are appealing and personal.

Watch for interesting seed pods, berries and grasses to combine with your flowers. There are endless varieties of grasses everywhere, varying in texture, form and tone of color.

These flowers and foliages will give you a diversified collection of dried materials from the entire growing season. Not only will you have a range of colors but also the many forms and shapes needed for interesting designs. Always dry flowers in various stages of growth —from buds to mature blooms—and dry twice as much as you will need. It is good to have extras to replace those broken or crushed and to freshen your arrangements from time to time.

PREPARING FLOWERS AND FOLIAGE FOR DRYING

Flowers to dry, like vegetables to freeze, must be picked at the proper time to insure good results. In other words, flowers should be at "peak of bloom," in prime condition when rich in color, never when faded and shedding petals (except for potpourri). Dry flowers as quickly as possible after picking to preserve color.

Pick flowers to dry on a warm, sunny day, never just after a rain. The afternoon when no dew is present is the best time. Choose blooms free from insect damage because this will definitely show after drying. Of course, if only one petal is damaged, either remove or reshape it with scissors.

Cut stems short—about one and one-half inches. There are several reasons for removing most of the natural stem. Practically all stems turn brown when dried, and are, therefore, not usable. The short stems will allow you to pack more flowers in the container and to store them better. Foliage should be removed and dried as individual leaves or sprays. Attach wire stems when you are ready to use your plant materials as explained in Chapter I.

PLANT MATERIALS FOR DRYING

Listed below are flowers and foliage that dry well. Do not limit yourself, however; I have never found a flower that will not dry with silica gel. If flowers and foliage in your locality are not included in this list, experiment and you will soon discover what dries best for you.

Acacia
Ageratum
Aster
Autumn Leaves
Baby's-Breath
Beech Foliage
Begonia (multiflora)
Bells of Ireland
Bridal Wreath
Butterfly-Bush Foliage
Calendula
Camellia
Candytuft
Canterbury Bells
Carnation
Chrysanthemum
Celosia
Columbine
Cornflower
Cosmos
Dahlia
Daisy
Delphinium
Deutzia
Dogwood
Dusty Miller (Artemisia)
Elaeagnus Foliage
Ferns: Maidenhair, Adiantum,
  Ocean Spray
Feverfew
Forget-me-not
Foxglove
Galax Leaves
Gardenia
Gladiolus
Heather
Honeysuckle Foliage
Hyacinth

Hydrangea
Iris Foliage
Ivy Leaves
Lamb's Ears (Stachys)
Lantana
Larkspur
Laurel Leaves
Lavender
Ligustrum Berries (Green)
Lilac
Lily-of-the-Valley
Lily-of-the-Valley Foliage
Lupine
Lupine Foliage
Marigold
Mullein
Nandina Berries
Nandina Foliage
Orchid
Pansy
Peony
Poppy Foliage
Ranunculus
Rose
Rose Foliage
Sage
Salvia
Scabiosa
Snapdragon
Snow-on-the-Mountain
  (sear the stems)
Spirea
Stock
Tassel-Flower
Tithonia
Viola
Zinnia

DRIED FLOWERS AFFECTED BY HUMIDITY

The flowers in this category will dry beautifully but because of their texture are likely to reabsorb moisture from the air and wilt. The drier the room, the longer they will last. Even if they last only a month, an early touch of spring makes the effort worthwhile. If these flowers are stored as soon as they are dried, in airtight Mason jars holding a couple of tablespoons of blued silica gel, they will keep indefinitely.

Anemone   Lily
Azalea   Scilla
Clematis   Snowdrop
Narcissus   Violet
Nasturtium

Note: Any flower with a sticky surface such as the petunia or nicotiana should not be dried because it is difficult to remove the silica gel.

SMALL FLOWERS

When you are planting your garden, remember to include miniature roses and zinnias, violas (Johnny-jump-up), forget-me-nots and lilies-of-the-valley. These flowers when dried are used in making greeting cards, paperweights, pictures and other small items. Of course, the florets of deutzia, hydrangea, lilac, delphinium and scilla will supply small forms. The velvet texture of celosia is lovely combined with any flower.

ROSETTE OF MULLEIN

For a distinctive center of interest for a wall plaque or flower arrangement, use a rosette of mullein. This weed is found along the roadside and in the fields in the early spring and again in the fall. The young sprouts of velvety green petals form the rosette. Pull the growth from the ground by the root and allow it to dry for several hours. When the leaves are limp, place the rosette in a cardboard box on crushed tissue paper. Arrange the leaves as you wish them to dry and place bits of facial tissue to support them in a natural position. Cover the entire rosette with several layers of tissue and allow to dry in a warm place for about two weeks. Use them in an arrangement as a soft grey-green point of interest or spray them gold for a festive note. Combine a rosette with pine lightly sprayed on the edges with gold for a very decorative effect.

III Interior Decorating with Natural Materials

As there are endless possibilities for using dried materials, it is the intention of this chapter not only to show accomplished creations, but also to kindle your own creativity. Look around you and see how many commercial articles may be given a priceless, hand-made look with dried flowers, seeds, pods, cones, shells and stones. Arrangements can be used, as they have been used here, to decorate walls, lamps, drawer pulls and mirrors; living room, bedrooms and kitchen. They can fill all of your rooms with a sense of nature, or they can be used sparingly to "immortalize" one or two favorite garden achievements. What a marvelous sense of continuity and purpose one gets from this final result of one's gardening efforts! Seeding, weeding, harvesting, drying and finally interior decorating—surely the life cycle of the flower has been prolonged to give almost endless pleasure!

WALL DECORATIONS

A wall is just a wall unless it gets special attention. Express your creative ability with wall hangings. Large or small, used inside or outside, they are extremely ornamental, fascinating to make and costing practically nothing. They can be constructed from odds and ends of lumber or from heavy fabrics. Here are some suggestions:

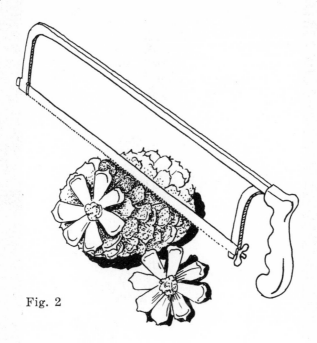

Fig. 2

PANELS FEATURING DRIED PLANT MATERIALS

Your background may be a wood panel, stained, waxed, painted or unfinished (only sanded to highlight the wood grain). A pair of wooden picnic plates make a handsome background.

Materials for the design may include vine tendrils such as wisteria; different sizes and varieties of seeds; seedpods of poppies, iris, hollyhocks and lilies; cones, berries, dried flowers and foliage. Pine cone rosettes are lovely and are made by sawing off slices of a cone as shown in Figure 2. If a saw is not available, you may remove the petals with a sharp knife and insert them into a tiny styrofoam ball; tint the center with brown shoe polish. For a holiday arrangement, apply glue to the petals, sprinkle with glitter and combine with fresh evergreens. Plate 8 shows a variety of seedpods combined with a rosette of mullein, dried according to the directions in Chapter II.

Your design may have a natural, unstudied effect like a vine trailing gracefully across the panel, or you may have a pure abstraction based on an interplay of forms and textures. Reds, yellows, greens,

even blues as well as subtle browns and grays may be included. Touches of black and off-white are useful for accent.

The material should be placed on the panel exactly as it is to appear when finished. With pencil, lightly mark the outline of the design. Remove the material and reassemble on a piece of cardboard. Begin with the main line of the design, gluing each piece in place. Fill in with long, narrow pods and foliage to create the outline or silhouette and complete the design with round shapes for the center of interest.

This same type of plaque or wall hanging may be made on heavy cardboard and covered with burlap or other suitable materials. Lightweight picture molding, glued on, will finish off the edges. Of course, old picture frames also may be used.

For bold color, try a red frame, with background of white burlap and zinnias in shades of pink to red. For exotic appeal on a background of gold velvet, use a dried wisteria branch with a hanging bunch of grapes made with acorns, or flowers formed from seeds. Color the dried materials with Treasure Jewel rub-on paint in blending tones. This type of paint is applied with finger or cloth, dries quickly and comes in an exquisite assortment of colors. It gives a permanent luster to almost any surface. (See Sources of Supply.)

VIII. (Opposite)   A wall panel such as this, with heavily textured seed pods and mullein rosette for a center of interest, is effective in informal rooms. There is virtually no limit to the materials you can use, nor the treatment you can give them. Wired nuts and cones add depth. They can be shellacked, waxed, gilded, painted or antiqued. Copper mesh screening makes a handsome background too. Be sure to select different shapes and textures to compensate for the muted color scheme.

BUTTERFLIES

Butterflies of velvet-textured celosia (Plate 9) can brighten the chimney breast in a playroom or be a gay addition to the breakfast nook. Glue a piece of lightweight cardboard to the back of the rattan frame and, when thoroughly dry, trim away the cardboard from the edges with a razor blade. Cut the celosia in small pieces and attach to the frame with glue. Highlight the spots of the butterfly with a single daisy or anemone. For more brilliance, fill the circles with colored stones, sequins or beads.

JAPANESE ROCKS

For an unusual wall decoration, paint several flat Japanese rocks in an appropriate color or leave them natural. With an electric drill, make a small hole at the top for hanging them on a screw or a cup hook. Or paste a tiny band of velvet ribbon, doubled over for hanging, to the back of the rock. Decorate the flat sides with tiny dried flowers. Try pale yellow rocks with tiny purple Johnny-jump-ups, violas or daisies, or shell pink rocks with blue forget-me-nots, deep pink roses and touches of dusty miller. These rocks are quite decorative grouped together on a coffee table or used as paperweights. Since a paperweight is handled frequently, dipping the decorated top in warm melted paraffin will make it more durable.

IX. (Opposite)   Butterflies of red celosia with jeweled ornaments make an interesting silhouette against a wall. They are charming also as a flower arrangement accessory.

The rooster (see Color Plate I and pattern on opposite page) is made from the following:

1. *Yellow Popcorn*
2. *Red Popcorn*
3. *Yellow-Gold Popcorn*
4. *Green Popcorn*
5. *Orange Popcorn*
6. *Small Cloves*
7. *Brown Cloves*
8. *Large Cloves for toes*
9. *Split Peas*
10. *Blue Popcorn*
11. *Red Kidney Beans*
12. *Speckled Butterbeans*
13. *Speckled Butterbeans*
14. *Pinto Beans*
15. *Baby Lima Beans*
16. *Great Northern Beans for background*

SEED MOSAICS

Wall hangings may start from seeds. The seed mosaic, Color Plate I, is a proud rooster made on a nineteen-by-twenty-six-inch cork bulletin board. Bright red, yellow and green popcorn combined with white and speckled butter beans and kidney beans provide the gay plumage. The background is made with Great Northern beans.

The choice of seeds for making mosaics is unlimited. To suggest a few which are readily available: corn, watermelon, pumpkin, lima bean, green bean, coffee, peanut, kidney bean, wheat, date, sunflower, pea, rice and muskmelon. Some may be painted dark with rub-on paint (see Sources of Supply) or dipped in Tintex. Before dyeing, soak seeds in warm water for a few minutes to soften the skins and allow the dye to penetrate. Make the dye solution strong, using warm, *not hot*, water and leave the seeds in for only a few minutes. Dry them on paper. For a gloss, spray dried seeds with clear plastic.

SHADES

If you have a window shade that remains half-way drawn, why not highlight it with a decorative picture of flowers? It could be just

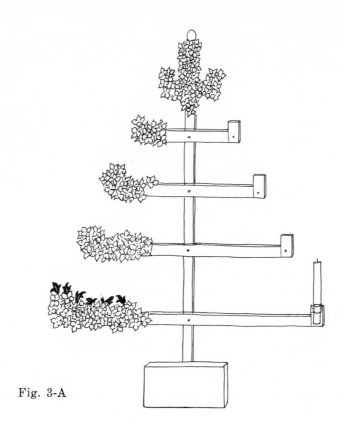

Fig. 3-A

a bouquet of mixed flowers related to a standing flower arrangement elsewhere in the room; or in a vase cut from felt or velvet-textured ribbon; or three felt flower pots containing topiary trees made of dried plant materials. Sketch your design first, remove the stems from the flowers and glue them in place. (See information on picture-making on page 56.) For a powder room, a peacock or a swan cut from white felt could be a container for roses, daisies, pansies, zinnias and blue cornflowers.

ESPALIERED TREE

Make an unusual and striking espaliered tree for a large brick or stone wall. Buy a wooden plant trellis or build a frame as shown in

Fig. 3-B

Figure 3-A and 3-B. Use a rectangular block of wood one-inch thick for the base. Stain or paint it a color and make it more ornate by gluing on pieces of broken glass of appropriate color. To the base, attach the center shaft and branches made from wooden strips one and one-fourth inches wide by one-half inch thick. For a more modern flair with turned-up branches, extend a short strip one and one-fourth inches on the ends as shown in the drawing.

At Christmas, tape on a small plastic medicine bottle to hold a candle. Insert an eye screw at the top for hanging and spray-paint the tree green. With fine wire, attach sprays of cedar and English ivy, laurel leaves or clusters of green hydrangea to the branches. You may glue the materials directly to the wooden frame, but wire can be easily removed and the tree redecorated to suit another occasion. Add wire stems to the flowers and attach by entwining the frame. For variety,

X.   *A bouquet of flowers, pressed and mounted on a soft yellow back-*
ground, with overlay mat of green, is framed in bamboo.

change the flowers from time to time using pink and white dogwood,
roses, marigolds, zinnias, cosmos, dahlias or asters. At Christmas,
hang decorated eggs or ornaments on the tree or trim it with fresh
holly and red velvet bows.

If you wish the tree free-standing, place the base stems in a large pot and fill with Sacrete mixed with water, following package directions, or with plaster of Paris. Place a layer of green moss on top. It will eventually dry and retain its green color indefinitely. For a smaller table model, twenty-eight inches high, use one-inch strips of wood.

PRESSED-FLOWER PICTURES

Use heavyweight drawing paper as the background for the picture. Plate 10. Either sketch your design first, or just lay down the materials, moving them around until you find a good arrangement. Then transfer the pressed flowers and leaves, one at a time, to another sheet of drawing paper, gluing each one down separately with Elmer's or Sobo glue. Cover with glass for protection. With freezer tape, attach a piece of thin plastic or heavy paper on the back of the frame to keep out dust and moisture. When you frame the picture, a colorful mat can be added to outline the pressed-flower design. Directions for drying the plant materials are given on page 28.

BOTANY FRAME

An oval botany frame as shown in Color Plate V is always eye-catching. These frames are very decorative and do not require many flowers. You can usually find them in florist and gift shops. To arrange, secure a tiny pinpoint holder to the recessed base of the frame with clay. Top the pinpoint with a piece of dry Oasis and insert the materials. You can use either one kind of flower with foliage, or an assortment of roses, pansies, lilies-of-the-valley, individual florets of blue hydrangea, a few small daisies, dusty miller and fern.

SHADOW BOXES

SARDINE CANS   Attractive for a narrow wall space are small shadow boxes made from sardine cans. Plate 11. With an ice pick, make two holes at the top for attaching ribbon for hanging. If you prefer, you may omit the ribbon and use a picture hook on the back. One can in the photograph is sprayed with a bright green paint. The cones, acorns and dried zinnia are sprayed white for a procelain effect. For Christmas, mount three cans on a hanging panel of bright red felt.

Use gold or pastel rub-on paint (Treasure Jewels—See Sources of Supply) on the cans for a more delicate touch. Decorate with violas, miniature roses, begonias (multiflora), ageratum and deutzia. Trim the edge of the can with gold beading. For a child's room, use small figures in the cans such as ballerinas or animals. These small pictures are also good for bazaars.

XI.   *A jaunty giraffe, a lovable angel and dried flowers which look fresh and bright are staged in sardine tins.*

Fig. 4

TISSUE BOX   A cardboard facial tissue box will make a pretty shadow box. Using the small size, spray the box a gold or pastel color for all occasions. Use green or red for more festive times. Decorate the interior with small flowers or pieces of material. A madonna from a Christmas card may be mounted in the background and encircled with tiny flowers. For extra sparkle, add glitter and jewels. Attach three shadow boxes to a panel of red or green felt and hang it on a door to express the holiday spirit. Try several on a mantel and use votive candles in front to cast a soft light on the interiors. As garden therapy, garden club members could use their artistic talents to make these attractive shadow boxes to brighten the day for hospital patients.

HANDMADE BOXES   For a large shadow box, one suitable for snap-dragons, roses, zinnias, dahlias, asters, celosias, cosmos, combined with dusty miller and foliage of wild honeysuckle, butterfly bush and English laurel, a depth of about four inches will be needed. Assemble four pieces of half-inch wood in the length and width desired, either square or rectangular. Figure 4. A lumber dealer will cut and assemble

Fig. 5

the pieces for you. (Or perhaps your husband will construct one for you—mine did.) For the back of the shadow box, use quarter-inch plywood and cover it with the material of your choice. Glue material in place along the edges. In the center, attach a piece of dry Oasis with two bands of freezer or masking tape. Before inserting flowers and foliage in the Oasis, make preliminary holes for wood screws in the four corners of the plywood backing. This will prevent jarring the flowers in your completed design while you are attaching the back to the frame. Glass to fit the box may be purchased from any hardware store. Attach the glass with plastic adhesive tape and glue a lightweight decorative molding around the edges for a more attractive framing.

This type of shadow box may be hung on the wall, placed on a piece of furniture or attached to legs to serve as an end table. Figure 5. For a bedroom, finish it in a pastel color and use dainty flowers such as lilies-of-the-valley, hyacinths, pansies, roses and daisies; for a den, a stained wood frame with a mat of colored burlap containing zinnias and marigolds in shades of red and yellow combined with brown dock would be warm and inviting. A frame of oak or walnut for the foyer, living room or dining area, arranged with carnations, roses, celosias, dahlias, white dogwood, green foliage and artificial fruit will make a handsome picture. A strip of concealed lighting, as shown in Figure 4, will illuminate the transparent loveliness of the dried flowers.

XII.   *A dainty lamp illuminates brilliant flowers cut from the garden
many seasons ago.*

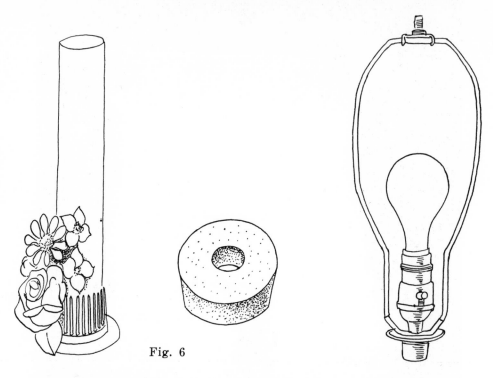

Fig. 6

MANTEL CLOCK

If you are fortunate and have or can find an old-fashioned mantel clock, whose days of keeping time are over, remove the mechanism and you will have a most unusual shadow box. Decorate the interior with flowers, cones and seed pods or with a collection of beach shells in a design. Wire it at the bottom for a small light bulb, which will cast a charming glow on the interior. Place it on the mantel or hang it in a hall to serve as a night light when needed.

LAMPS

A straight-sided glass container such as is used for bubble bath, guest soap and terrariums or a clear glass vase will make an unusual lamp base for displaying the dried flowers. Plate 12. The electric lamp adapters are available at hardware and ten-cent stores. Firmly press a cardboard tube (from a roll of paper towels or a mailing tube) onto a weighted pinpoint holder and paint both the tube and holder to blend with the flowers you are using. Figure 6. Glue the flowers directly to the tube, keeping in mind the inside dimension of the jar to allow

XIII.   Seeds, kidney beans and shells collected by children are an enduring delight when used to decorate a lamp for their own room.

clearance when you insert the arrangement. Holding the top of the tube, carefully slip it into the jar. To hold the lamp adapter, cut either a circle of wood about three-fourths of an inch thick or styrofoam one inch thick, to serve as a stopper. Make a hole in the center of the stopper to hold the adapter. Paint the outside wall of the stopper to blend with the flowers since it will show through the glass container. The shade may be further decorated if you so desire. In making your lamp base, choose flowers to harmonize with the furnishings. Try a combination of green hydrangea with pink or blue asters; yellow marigolds and brown dock; red zinnias and orange celosias.

A glass apothecary jar filled only with blue hydrangea makes a pretty base. Also, a pottery vase or jug with a lamp adapter and decoration on the outside is quite unique. Plate 13. Try a mullein rosette, cones, seed pods and brown dock on a yellow vase or a tan jug.

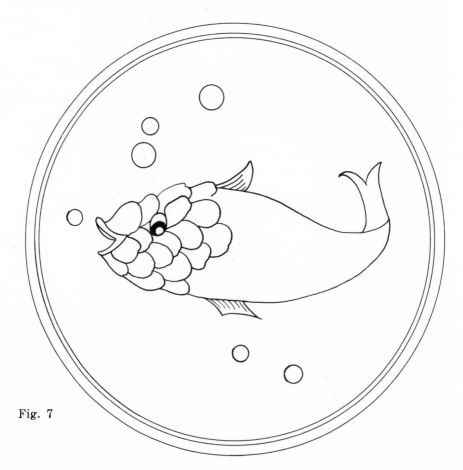

Fig. 7

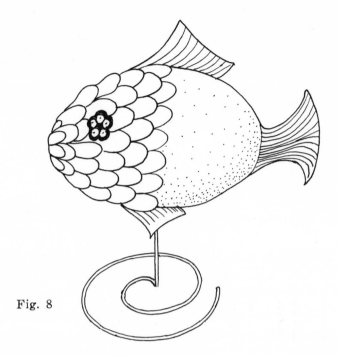

Fig. 8

POWDER ROOM

Paint several bottles in attractive shapes and decorate them with a few dried flowers. Before gluing, dip the flowers in melted paraffin (see page 27) and allow them to dry. This coating of wax will not only make the flowers more durable, but also protect them from the moisture usually existing in the powder room. Add a covered soap dish decorated in the same manner.

FISH PLAQUE

For a bathroom wall, hang a fish plaque fashioned of rose petals. Figure 7. Use an inexpensive, metal-edged asbestos hot plate as the background. Paint the mat with a flat finish in harmonizing color. With pencil, lightly outline the fish design. For relief, pad the body of the fish with a little cotton glued in place. To make the rose petals less brittle and more easily handled, dip them in warm melted paraffin and allow to dry. Glue petals on the design to simulate scales. For the fins, cut paper of matching color in thin strips and attach to the body with glue. Use a circle of dark sequins for the eye. Add a few circles of colored foil for bubbles.

A MOBILE   For an eye-catching mobile, make a complete fish from the large styrofoam egg form found in hobby stores and suspend it from the ceiling on fine wire. The oval shape is perfect for the body. Cover with rose petals, graduating them in size toward the head. Add paper fins and a circle of sequins for the eyes. If you prefer, mount the fish on a stand made of wire as shown in Figure 8.

BEDROOM ACCESSORIES

A HAT FOR THE WALL   Remember that dear little face under her very first hat? Cherish the memory and the treasure by decorating the hat with a circle of flowers to adorn the wall of a child's room. Plate 14. For a teenager, decorate her colorful beach hat in the same manner with dried seaweed, flowers and shells. She will love this souvenir from a wonderful trip to the shore!

PICTURES   What could be lovelier for the bedroom than a pair of flower pictures framed in gold and matted on velvet, or a fabric to harmonize with the décor? Plate 14. Search your attic or the antique store for old frames, or buy inexpensive ones from the ten-cent stores. Frames with a depth of about one inch are good, especially if you wish to cover the flowers with glass. Usually the cardboard back is strong enough to hold a fabric mat. Velvet, of course, makes a most elegant background for the flowers. In the photograph, the oval outline was made with gold braid. To create depth, place the flowers slightly higher in the center (use a little cotton padding if necessary) and gradually lower the materials as you reach the edges. Remove the stems and use glue to attach all materials. I always work out a design on paper before starting a picture.

A velvet frame, such as used for small photographs, can be decorated with dried flowers. Plate 14. Simply remove the metal-ringed cover, fill in the background with pastel paper or velvet and attach miniature flowers. Try a single pansy of different colors with a sprig

XIV. (Opposite)   Winter comes and goes and flowers still "bloom" on this child's hat, in framed pictures, and as decorative drawer pulls.

of fern in each opening, or an assortment of small flowers as shown in the photograph.

DRAWER PULLS   Perk up a chest in the guest room with flower-decorated drawer pulls. Plate 14. The hardware stores offer a wide selection of concave pulls. Some wooden ones have a recessed center of one-fourth of an inch. Fill the center with small flowers. For durability, dip the flower part *quickly* in warm melted paraffin after attaching the materials with glue. Hold it upside-down for a minute to thoroughly drip off the excess and to let it harden. Try just one flower, such as a blue aster, or several blossoms of double larkspur on a white chest. For a boy's room or the den, fill the center with acorns and tiny pine cones. Plate 14. Stain or paint the pull to harmonize with the chest. A single pansy or daisy can be permanently embedded in metal concave pulls with liquid plastic. (See Sources of Supply.)

MIRROR   Dress-up your mirror with net and flowers. Plate 15. It may be an easel type of mirror or one which hangs on the wall. Gather a three-inch strip of net down the middle, fold in half, and glue around the frame. Decorate with clusters of flowers.

PINCUSHION   Add a dainty pincushion to your dresser. Plate 15. Use a two-and-one-half inch styrofoam ball, cut about halfway through to the center, and glue it in a glass caster cup. Spray with paint in your choice of color. Fully gather one-half yard of satin ribbon three-fourths of an inch wide and encircle the styrofoam, holding the ribbon in place with pins as you glue it down. (When dry, remove the pins.) Trim with small flowers and tiny bows of ribbon. This is a good bazaar item, easy to make and appealing.

A FAN   To add a feminine touch to a night table or dresser, use Elmer's or Sobo adhesive to attach roses, hydrangeas, daisies, pansies, dusty miller and fern to the base of an open fan. Finish with a bow of velvet ribbon. The fan may be painted a delicate color or sprayed gold and held in position on a small plate stand. A pair of larger fans decorated in the same manner are quite lovely placed on each end

XV.   (Opposite)   The fairest flowers of them all are reflected in a mirror standing or on a wall. The pincushion is a match for it.

of a mantel. For the sentimentalist, flowers from a special occasion, such as a first prom, may be used to decorate the fan or a jewelry, cigarette or makeup box. Plate 16. Unfinished boxes of suitable sizes are available at hobby stores. Paint the box an appropriate color and decorate the top as shown in the photograph. For more glamour, line the interior of the box with velvet or satin.

XVI.   He said it with flowers—and here is the memory of that occasion.

IV   Long-Lasting Table
      Decorations

FOR A TABLE

Rose Trees using just roses or a variety of dried flowers are decorative
and easily made. Plate 17. Insert a slim wooden dowel in a styrofoam
ball, then insert the opposite end in a piece of styrofoam firmly
wedged in a flower pot or urn. (A ball of Tacky Tape in the bottom
of the container will hold it more securely.) Cover with green moss.
Break round toothpicks in half and cut small pieces of fine wire.
(Spools of wire may be obtained from any hardware store.) Cut three-
inch squares of nylon net; pinch together at the center and attach to
broken end of toothpicks by wrapping tightly with piece of wire. Insert
pointed end of toothpicks into styrofoam ball to cover it completely.
Tuck flowers in the folds of net or wire flowers to toothpicks and
insert. For a truly delicate effect, try color schemes of moss green
net with pink roses or soft yellow net with daisies and purple pansies.
Add green velvet or satin leaves for a note of elegance. These trees
are eye-catching for a dining table or buffet, and add charm to any
bedroom. Make a pair of trees with moss green net and change the
flowers for a formal or informal occasion. Six- to eight-inch trees,
trimmed with miniature roses, are attractive anywhere. Plate 17.
Here the round head of white hydrangea (paniculata grandiflora) is
attached with glue to the top of a small dowel and miniature pink
roses are inserted between the florets. Small pieces of blue hydrangea

XVII. *(Opposite)   Large or small, trees made with tufts of net and dried flowers which have kept their natural brilliance will brighten dreary days.*

XVIII. *(Below)   Pretty flowers sparkling under candlelight make a romantic setting for a party.*

may also be attached to a two-inch styrofoam ball with hairpins and this placed on a dowel. Trim with small flowers.

CANDELABRA

For a formal dinner or buffet, arrange flowers and foliage in the center of a candelabra as shown in Plate 18. Some candelabras have a stationary dish, while others can hold an epergnette in the candle socket. Attach two one-inch pinpoint holders with clay to each side of the central socket and firmly secure a piece of dry Oasis on the points. Outline edge of the container with dusty miller, grasses and lily-of-the-valley leaves. Fill in with blue and green hydrangea, roses, larkspurs, anemones, ageratum, hardy begonias and pansies. If after use you wish to store your candelabra, carefully lift the pinpoint holders and place the arrangement in a plastic bag until you need it again.

DISH GARDEN

Interesting, pleasing and lasting is a dish garden made of dried flowers and therefore requiring no maintenance. The simple, woodsy composition in Plate 19 contains ledge rock in various brown tones, maidenhair fern, Virginia heart leaf, green moss, a few white violets and scillas for a touch of spring. Since violets and scilla are likely to be affected by humidity, they received a dipping of warm melted paraffin for protection as explained on page 27.

QUICKIE CENTERPIECES

For an informal luncheon or dinner, arrange small flowers or just one flower on a one-inch square of Oasis, place on a saucer or plate of blending color and cover with a hurricane chimney. Around the edge of the plate use pieces of fresh cedar or other greens. When candles are desired, use the chimneys to cover the candles and encircle the plate with dried flowers. Use several decorations down the length of the table, or group three together as a centerpiece.

When unexpected dinner guests arrive, quickly make a fresh and appealing centerpiece with red apples and dried flowers. On a footed

XIX.   This dish garden made of earthy materials and a few bright blossoms requires no maintenance.

dish, stack apples in a pyramid, holding them together with toothpicks. Using freezer tape, attach a short piece of wire to small clusters of blue hydrangea and white daisies and tuck flowers between the apples. Add a little fresh or dried foliage in the same manner. Substitute artificial apples if you wish and use Tacky Tape to keep them stacked.

DOGWOOD BRANCH

If you grow dogwood, be sure to dry a supply of blooms. The flowers dry beautifully and can be used for many decorations. By attaching the blooms to a dried branch, you can create the effect of a living branch of dogwood. Plate 20. Attach the branch to a free-form base of wood and use brown floral tape for attaching the flowers. Tint the base and branch with brown shoe polish for an even, natural effect. Interesting branches may be found in the woods or manzanita branches and free-form bases may be obtained from gift stores or garden centers. For a more delicate effect, spray the branch and base white. Use white tape to attach the dogwood blossoms. At Christmas or Easter, the same white branch may display decorated eggs. For Easter, place little chicks in a nest of paper excelsior around the base.

GLASS DOMES

The tall, elegant table decoration in Color Plate III shows a tiered arrangement of brandy snifters in graduated sizes. A glass cake stand serves as the base. Starting with the arrangement for the large size bowl, cover a one-inch pinpoint holder with a two-inch block of Oasis. Insert a six-inch wooden pick in the center of the block making certain it is securely wedged in the pinpoint holder. This pick will serve as a handle to lower the finished arrangement into the bowl. The flowers and foliage in the arrangement will hide the pick from view. From the hardware store, have pieces of glass cut to fit the tops of the bowls. Follow the same procedure for the next two bowls, decreasing the size of the Oasis and the arrangement, and the length of the wooden pick. Finish with the top of a candy jar of clear glass. Colored or clear marbles, stacked to form a peak, are also an effective top. Figure 9. A touch of glue on the marbles will hold them in place. If this arrangement is to be used for the holidays, use Christmas balls instead of marbles. Place a circle of fresh or dried foliage around the edge of each tier.

XX.   (Opposite)   Spring is here! Preserved dogwood blossoms added to bare branches and a few decorated eggs welcome Easter.

How handsome this would be centered on a buffet! For a banquet table, it could be repeated at properly spaced intervals down the length of the table. Single snifters could be used on the smaller tables. I am sure the guests will be entranced, and best of all, the centerpieces can be done long in advance.

Display your "blue ribbon" rose, dahlia or other specimen under glass. Figure 10. Dry the flower according to directions, place it on a round glass ash tray or caster cup and invert a brandy snifter or any goblet large enough to cover it. Stack a few marbles on top, as described above, for a knob effect. With this top trimming of glass marbles, a plain glass is transformed to a most unique dome.

This display will be an "eye-catcher" on a desk, on coffee or end tables or anywhere! Use several, each with a different flower under its

Fig. 9   Fig. 10

Fig. 11

glass, down the middle of a narrow table or in a circle for a center-piece. If you wish candlelight, use votive candles on top of the inverted glass. Figure 10. Add a few sprays of English ivy around the base. Spray the ivy with Seymour's Clear Plastic Spray #11-821 to give it a luster similar to glass.

Dry very special flowers from your garden. When the occasion arises to visit a sick friend, place a flower with a little foliage inside a glass, lightly apply glue around the top edge and stretch Saran Wrap across the opening to completely cover. Cut the wrap, leaving one-eighth of an inch over lapping, and cover it with a band of ribbon glued in place. Finish with a small bow.

Stemmed glasses from the dime store, when filled with dried flowers, make a charming favor for luncheons. Nice for use as place cards too.

PLASTIC BALLS

Small, clear plastic balls that fit together are a pretty way to display single flowers. Figure 11. (See Sources of Supply.) The balls have a small plastic loop for hanging. For standing, glue a plastic ring to the bottom of the ball to keep it from rolling. As a therapy project, Garden Club members could use this attractive means of taking their garden flowers to hospital patients during the winter months.

NOSEGAYS

Nosegay decorations (see Chapter VII) enhance a table any time. For more color, add lavender scillas, clusters of blue forget-me-nots and, for highlight, a few white daisies. Make up several at the beginning of winter and store them in airtight plastic bags, so table decorations are always ready. For a spring Garden Club luncheon, nothing would be more appropriate. For a guest to enjoy, place one on a bedside table or dresser.

V   Dried Decorations for Christmas and Other Occasions

CHRISTMAS TREE

A Christmas tree of felt, adorned with dried flowers, makes a charming hanging decoration. Figure 12. Use it in your home, take it to mother, or give it to a shut-in to brighten his room. The felt tree may be mounted on cardboard or, if unmounted, may be rolled up, stored away and redecorated the next year.

Cut the tree and tub from one piece of felt, making it about thirty-three inches in all. Cover the trunk and tub with contrasting colors. For instance, use green felt for the tree and white for the trunk and tub. Trim with gold rickrack, either stitching or gluing it to the felt. Scatter dried white dogwood blossoms and red velvet bows over the tree. For variation, use a pink tree and white trunk and tub, decorating with daisies and red roses.

DECORATED BELLS

Dress up the inside doors throughout the house with bells covered with dried flowers. Figure 13. Cut the bell form from cardboard, pad or quilt it slightly around the center area with cotton, and glue on flowers to completely cover the surface. On a bedroom door, use blue hydrangea with a red rose clapper; for the foyer, cover a bell with red celosia, using a gold Christmas ball for the clapper; for the den or playroom door, cover the bell with yellow marigolds with a green ball clapper. Finish the top of the bell with a matching ribbon bow. Use three matching bells together or let them sway singly from a gilded rope.

PANELS

The hanging in Figure 14 is suitable for a wall or door. To make, cut a piece of felt twelve-by-thirty-three inches in your choice of color. Turn a one-inch hem at the top and bottom of the panel and either stitch or glue to form a casing for two short brass curtain rods. Using a rod in the bottom hem will add weight to keep the panel straight. Glue on three six-inch gold, silver or white paper doilies. Add flowers

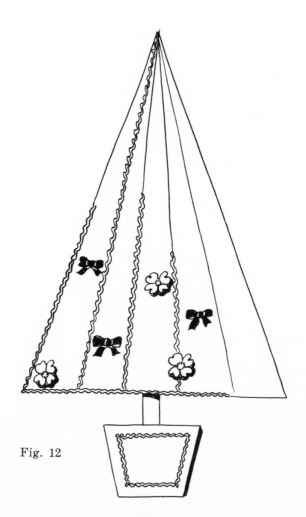

Fig. 12

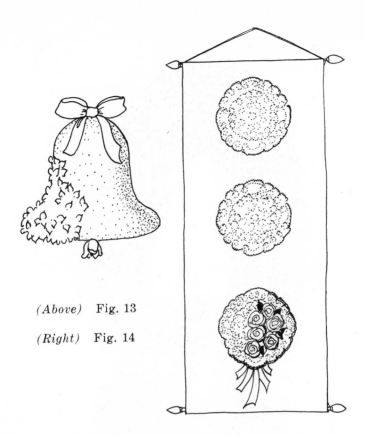

(Above)   Fig. 13

(Right)   Fig. 14

and foliage to form a nosegay and finish with several pieces of ribbon. For a smaller space, make a panel eight-by-nineteen inches and use four-inch doilies and miniature flowers.

STOCKINGS

For His and Her stockings, cut the designs from felt and glue to a cardboard backing. Make Hers in shocking pink with a garter at the top of lace, ribbon, flowers and tiny Christmas ornaments. His could be in green with toe and heel covered with white dogwood. Finish the top with a red bow and more blossoms.

MADONNA IN A NICHE

Containers, containers everywhere! Just glance around your house, and you will find them in every shape and form.

XXI.   The interior of a ham can is the unusual niche for a serene Madonna and a long-lasting floral design.

The pear-shaped ham can sprayed gold, has a blue velvet background glued to the inside. Plate 21. Red roses and sprays of dusty miller surround the small Madonna. This shadow box may be hung on the wall by gluing a small picture hook on the back. Since the bottom is flat, however, it could be free-standing. Make one for the kitchen with a candle to serve as a reserve light if electricity fails. Paint outside of can black, with a red interior, and trim the opening with black cotton fringe. Use a red votive candle at the base and decorate with white pine cone flowers.

CHRISTMAS TRIMMINGS

Christmas balls that have lost their luster may become lovelier than ever. Spray the balls with flat paint in soft pastels. Starting at the top, glue on several uneven pieces of narrow satin or velvet ribbon. Glue dried miniature roses, Johnny-jump-ups, florets of lilac, forget-me-not, bridal wreath and larkspur in place around the top and cascade them slightly down the sides of the balls. For a mobile effect, hang several balls on fine wire from the ceiling in a corner of the room.

Mobiles are so fascinating—here is another one. Cut a two-inch circle of lightweight cardboard, make a small hole near the edge and attach fine wire for hanging. Glue a four-inch gold or silver paper doily on each side of the cardboard circle. Pad the center with cotton and arrange small flowers and fern in a nosegay design on both sides. The center thickness will create a ball effect that may be viewed from all sides. Attach wire to the ceiling with freezer tape and cover with a small bow lightly glued to the tape.

XXII.   A parade of real and plastic foam eggs decorated with plant materials for Easter or Christmas includes a nativity scene.

DECORATIVE EGGS

Plastic-foam eggs, real egg shells and the panorama (see Sources of Supply) shown in Plate 22, delicately tinted and decorated, make delightful gifts for the Easter and Christmas seasons. Adorn them with tiny Peruvian starflowers, gold braid, sparkling jewels, seed pearls and other trinkets found around the house. They are fun for the whole family to make. The panorama has four cut-out windows. The openings may contain a tiny arrangement of flowers, a peaceful scene, or a miniature animal in a natural setting. Children especially enjoy making these panoramas. Glue on three small wooden balls for the feet or, if you wish to hang it, insert a wire hook at the top.

Hobby stores have foam eggs in pastel colors or white ones for you to tint. Of course, real egg shells are readily available and can be decorated in the same manner. Directions for removing the contents of an egg are:

Shake the egg a few times to loosen the membrane. Make a pin-hole in each end and blow the contents into a bowl. If you have trouble removing the contents, enlarge the holes slightly and insert a fine wire into the egg to further loosen the contents. When the egg is completely blown out, rinse it well in a bowl of water and drain it thoroughly. If the egg is to be hung, insert the two ends of a loop of thread into the hole at the small end before decorating the egg. With a toothpick, apply glue to form a layer over the entire openings.

If you wish to decorate the interior of the egg, draw an oval outline on the side of the egg, and using an ice pick, gently pierce a hole in the center. Make a pinhole in the small end of the egg for the hanging thread. Use sharp manicure scissors to cut around edge of oval, starting from the hole in the center. Remove the contents, thoroughly clean the shell and drain. Dip the shell in a dye bath of vegetable coloring or egg dye. Let the shell dry. Follow the directions above for attaching a loop of thread for hanging. To preserve the shell, coat the inside with clear nail polish. Decorate the interior with tiny angels, animals, shells or dried flowers, gluing the items in place. A small Madonna cut from a Christmas card, placed at the back of your design, will make a lovely point of interest. Trim the edge of the opening as suggested above. Goose or duck eggs make beautiful standing ornaments. Fasten these decorative eggs to manzanita branches for an interesting centerpiece. Plate 20.

CANDLES

A burning candle is a symbol of spiritual light. Decorated candles add charm not only at Christmas but throughout the year. Only paraffin and simple items from the kitchen are needed to make a variety of shapes. For molds, use milk cartons in all sizes, cardboard mailing tubes, juice-concentrate cans and glass bottles.

The paraffin may be used white or tinted with all-purpose dyes. Because of the density of the wax, the lighter dyes produce brighter shades in the paraffin. Light green, chartreuse, yellow, evening blue and coral are recommended. Use one to two teaspoons of Rit dye for each pound of paraffin. One pound fills three 6-ounce juice-concentrate cans. One-and-three-fourths pounds fills a one-quart milk carton. In using cardboard mailing tubes, cut them in desired lengths and glue a piece of cardboard to the bottom. With a knitting needle, punch a hole in the bottom and using heavy string for a wick; thread it through, allowing a half-inch to overlap; hold it in place with adhesive tape. Secure the string at the top by wrapping it around a pencil and placing it across the top of the container. Completely melt the paraffin in a double boiler, or improvise with a large fruit juice can set in a pan of water. Stir in all-purpose dye. Remove from boiling water and stir thoroughly for three to five minutes. Some of the dye will not entirely dissolve, but the residue will settle to the bottom of the melted wax. The paraffin also may be tinted with stubs of old candles of one color or colored crayons. Let the colored wax cool a bit before pouring into the mold. Allow about twelve hours to thoroughly harden. To remove candles, peel off the milk cartons or other cardboard molds. Dip metal molds in hot water to loosen. Trim the wick at the bottom, leaving about one inch at the top for lighting.

Glass bottles of unusual shapes make interesting candles. Drop the wick into the bottle, securing it to the bottom with a drop or two of paraffin and at the top as previously described. Pour in the wax and allow to harden. To remove, score the bottle down the center with a glass cutter, place in a paper bag and tap it with a hammer until glass breaks away from the wax. Trim the wick to the proper length.

A "snow coating" may be added to your candles with whipped wax. To make, pour melted wax into a bowl and allow to cool until a film forms over the top. Using a fork, gently beat until foamy like a frosting and quickly spoon it onto the outside of the candles in successive coats. Reheat and rebeat if it starts to thicken.

To decorate, dip dried flowers in the melted paraffin (soft to touch) and allow them to dry. When ready to apply, dip the backs of flowers and foliage in the melted wax and affix to the candles in an appropriate design. For more dazzling decorations, gems, sequins and glitter may be added with glue. Plate 23 shows several examples of decorated candles.

XXIII.   From bottle shapes and cartons come homemade candles. They are trimmed with a variety of materials to suit your fancy.

MAKING DECORATIONS FOR PARTIES

With a good supply of dried materials, you can make artistic decorations for special occasions well in advance or on short notice. Your flowers may be used time and time again. They can be returned to storage after the party to await another call to service.

VALENTINE'S DAY

An empty box of Valentine candies makes the sentimental "Hearts and Flowers" table decoration in Plate 24. The box top is padded lightly with cotton and covered with pink velvet. A three-inch strip of pink net, gathered and folded down the center, is attached to the edge of the box with glue. The outside heart design is made of blue hydrangea. The gathered net is repeated on the inside heart and the center is filled with roses, larkspurs, zinnias, celosias, daisies, deutzia, statice, dusty miller and fern. The heart is held in position on a plate stand.

XXIV.   For sweet and treasured memories, make a lacy heart and adorn it with delicate flowers for Valentine's Day or another romantic occasion.

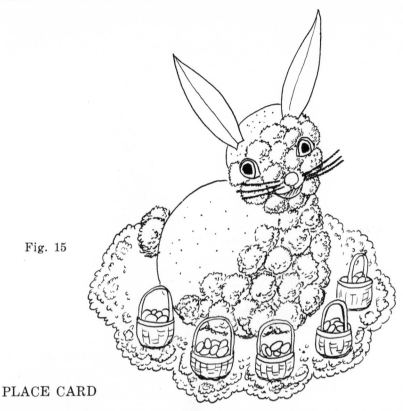

Fig. 15

PLACE CARD

The heart place card is outlined with gold braid and is trimmed with a tiny rose bud.

EASTER

Children will enjoy the party rabbit shown in Figure 15. Shape an oval piece of Oasis for the body and a round piece for the head. Join the two pieces with small picks. Using pink carnations, celosia or small white chrysanthemums, cover the entire body and head. Cut the facial features from construction paper and glue them in place. Add white pipe cleaners for the whiskers. Place the bunny on a large lace doily for the centerpiece and surround it with small baskets of jelly beans for the guests.

HALLOWEEN

A cat's head, formed of bright yellow or orange marigolds, will make an intriguing centerpiece for Halloween. Figure 16. Join two pieces

Fig. 16

of Oasis with small florist picks and round off to make a ball six inches in diameter. Flatten one side slightly for the bottom area. Cover the entire ball with marigolds. Make ears, eyes and nose from black construction paper, attaching them with glue. Insert black pipe cleaners for the whiskers. (Dye white ones black with shoe polish.) Place the head on a scalloped, sixteen-inch circle of black oilcloth. For an eerie setting, burn low candles in tin cans, painted black and pierced with holes. Use a small scalloped oilcloth mat under the cans.

The Halloween and Easter ideas may be adapted for a wall hanging. Using a painted, round, asbestos mat, draw the design and pad the center lightly with cotton for relief. With glue, attach dried orange marigolds for the cat's head and small white chrysanthemums for the rabbit. Follow the previous suggestions for the facial features. These are quickly made for children's parties. Hang them on the wall above the party table or use them on a plate stand for the centerpiece. After the party, they can be enjoyed as wall decorations in the children's rooms.

THANKSGIVING

Suggestive for Thanksgiving is the flower-decorated turkey in Plate 25. To make, remove the pointed top of a pine cone to get a flat surface for the breast. Wrap a piece of wire around the cone and shape it for the neck and head in proportion to the body. Glue cotton onto the wire,

XXV.   This perky turkey with his colorful plumage of orange and yellow marigolds can decorate your table for many Thanksgiving feasts.

*XXVI.   A pine cone tree with preserved flowers can be made weeks ahead
for Thanksgiving or Christmas.*

making it *double* thickness to allow for shrinkage of the cotton when
you apply brown shoe polish to color. Use black buttons for the eyes
and red strips of leather for the wattles. For the legs and feet, wrap
a long piece of heavy wire around the back part of the cone and bend
forward to form the feet. Cover the legs and feet with yellow wool
or raffia. Decorate with yellow, orange and red marigolds or other
dried flowers in autumn colors.

Once you have your turkey made, you can store and use him at
any time. If marigolds or small mums are still blooming, wrap a little
piece of wet cotton around the stems and insert between the pine
petals. Or, buy a few yellow carnations from the florist, split them
carefully and then wrap the petals with wet cotton; cover with floral

tape and use for your flowers. Small mums from the florist are quite inexpensive and may be used in the same fashion. Place the turkey, without flowers, on top of a mound of fresh or artificial fruit for a large, attractive centerpiece.

A giant pine cone also makes a colorful tree for Thanksgiving. Plate 26. For the base and trunk, insert a long screw up through first a block of wood, then a spool and finally into the bottom of the cone. A long nail will also go through the base and spool and into a small disc of wood one-fourth of an inch thick; to this disc glue the pine cone. Paint the base and trunk dark brown. Between the petals, use small artificial fruit and shellacked or painted acorns and pods. For an all-season decoration, spray the pine cone green and tuck flowers between the petals. For a more delicate tree, spray the cone, base and trunk white. At Christmas, decorate with balls, trinkets and jewels.

BABY SHOWER

Cut a stork from heavy cardboard of the type used for posters. Figure 17. Use a short florist pick, rounded off and painted pink, for the bill and two long picks for the legs. Attach the picks to the cardboard in the proper position with freezer or masking tape. Using glue, pad both sides of the stork with cotton for body thickness. Lightly apply glue to the cotton and completely cover with blue or white hydrangea. Add a few blue or white feathers for the tail. Hobby stores carry small packages of feathers in many colors. A black button will serve as an eye. Insert the leg picks in a weighted pinpoint holder. Cover the holder with shredded paper or tufts of net for the nest. Enclose a tiny plastic baby in a square of net and hang from the bill, holding it in place with glue.

SWEET SIXTEEN

"Sugar and spice and everything nice." With this theme, a simple but pretty table can be decorated with spicy pomanders, later to be given to the guests as favors. Plate 27. For the base, use a three-inch circle of styrofoam about one-inch thick. With tiny balls of Tacky Tape, attach lumps of sugar around the base. (Later they can be removed and used.) Add tufts of net around the edge, tuck in sprigs of fresh boxwood, and round pastel mints for the flowers. The pomanders can

Fig. 17

be made months before the special occasion. Here are the directions: Using oranges, lemons, limes or juicy apples, pierce the fruit with an ice pick, just deep enough to insert whole cloves, and cover completely as shown in the photograph. The juicier the fruit, the better, for the fixative is absorbed by the juice and the fragrance of the fruit and cloves will last longer. For the fixative, use powdered orris root mixed with a little cinnamon or scented sandalwood. Sprinkle the powder over the stuffed fruit using as much as it will take up. Allow the fruit to dry thoroughly which usually takes at least a month. If the fixative

XXVII.   "Sugar and spice and everything nice." Fragrant pomanders convey the message.

powder appears thick or caked after the fruit is dried, remove the excess with a small vegetable brush. Place the dried pomander on a square of colored net and bringing it up around the ball, tie with decorative gold cord or ribbon to form the hanger. A small cluster of antiqued flowers or tiny gold-sprayed pine cones make pretty trimmings.

These spicy pomanders, used in closets for a delightful fragrance, make an attractive and useful gift. They are always popular at a bazaar.

VI   Unique Articles to Wear

DRIED-FLOWER HAT

Surprise the girls at the Garden Club luncheon with a hat of dried flowers and foliage. Color Plate II. I promise you many compliments. Not only will it create exclamations of delight, but it's so much fun to make.

Lacy hat frames, like the one I have used, come in soft pastels. You may also use a white buckram frame. Both may be purchased from the ten-cent or fabric stores. Choose a becoming style in a white buckram frame and cover it completely with an assortment of garden flowers. Or paint the buckram frame any color you wish and use only a circle of flowers around the crown. Clip off the stems of the flowers and glue in place. For a wispy touch, add a few tufts of net in a harmonizing color. Spray the finished hat several times with Seymour's Clear Plastic Spray #11-821, allowing fifteen minutes drying time between sprayings. If the wind is blowing when you wear your hat, protect the flowers with a fine hair net or with a complete covering of a circle of net.

When your Flower Show schedule says "anything goes" or "the sky is the limit," why not enter a flowered hat of your creation? You will surely carry home a blue ribbon! Save your hat and perch it on a hat stand in your bedroom to add flowers in a novel fashion. Good for an Easter table centerpiece too.

HAIR ORNAMENTS

For that special party, wear flowers in your hair—dried ones from your garden. Color Plate II. Chignon spears are not only novel, but they are attractive and gay. Untrimmed plastic spears are found in the ten-cent stores. Attach a little cotton to the tops with glue and wrap with green floral tape to form a padding. Or, use large hairpins and make a padding at the arc by wrapping downward about six times around with tape, or until one inch of the top is covered. To this padding, attach the flowers with glue. A hair comb can be decorated in the same manner. To complement a black sheath, use a lovely red rose on a leaf of lily-of-the-valley; for a dainty ensemble, a circle of gathered net filled with florets of blue delphinium. Since you are using dried flowers you don't have to worry that they will die during the evening.

WATCH CASE

Among your possessions perhaps you have a locket, brooch or an unused watch. Have a jeweler remove the works of the watch and this will leave a shell for a delicate design. Color Plate II. For this unusual accessory, cut a piece of velvet to fit inside of watch case and glue in place. Start with a miniature rose (or any small flower) in the center and green fern outlining the edge. Work outward, gluing in place single florets of forget-me-not, bridal wreath, purple statice, miniature roses and small pieces of pink celosia. Separate the colors with tiny buds of dusty miller. Worn with a chain or watch fob pin, it will be a topic of conversation!

To complement the locket, brooch or watch, make matching earrings by gluing small flowers to earring forms which may be purchased from the ten-cent stores. These items can be especially personal if the flowers come from your garden.

Corsages are always lovely. Make them as long in advance as you like without worrying that they will wilt. You can also make a few to have on hand for last-minute gifts, in assorted colors, so you can pick one in harmony with the costume of the woman who is to receive it.

Give the hair ornaments and corsages several light sprayings with Seymour's Clear Plastic Spray #11-821 for protection from the weather.

VII   Here Comes the Bride

The bride is allergic to fresh flowers! Never mind, she may still carry the traditional wedding bouquet. Even her attendant can have a matching one. Bouquets and table arrangements can be planned and made months ahead at practically no cost and, if the flowers grew in the parents' garden, the sentiment makes the floral decorations even more cherished.

MAKING THE BRIDAL BOUQUET

Color Plate VII. Sew a half-circle of lightweight cardboard to a fan with an eighteen-inch spread at the top. (This will protect fan for later use.) Gather two yards of lace and satin ribbon and sew to the fan. Glue dried mock-orange blossoms, roses, carnations, scillas, daisies and maidenhair fern in place as shown in the picture. Add the wedding ribbon with streamers, tied with lover's knots.

MAKING A BRIDAL NOSEGAY

Color Plate VII. The bride in pink carries a nosegay centered with a pink carnation, encircled with pink rose buds, tufts of net, baby's breath and touches of green foliage. To make, use a florist's lace nosegay cup, a paper-lace doily or just gather lace or net to a circle

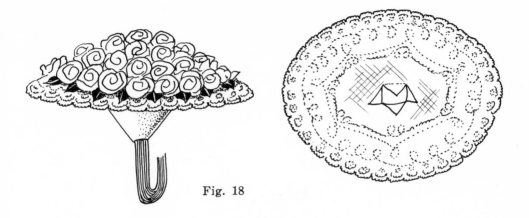

Fig. 18

of plastic (it is more durable than paper). Figure 18. If you make your nosegay cup, cut a cross in the center and bend the four V-shaped pieces under, later tacking them to the wire stems when you have finished the nosegay. At intervals, glue the leaves close to the edge of the lace circle. Add a few pieces of green hydrangea in the same manner. Wire the carnation, rose buds and tufts of net individually and wrap each stem with white floral tape. Arrange the flowers in a circle and insert the stems through the center opening of the nosegay cup. Tack the cup underneath to the wire stems, bend wire stems upward, press together, and wrap with tape. This will make one strong stem for the bride to hold the nosegay. Attach a bow and streamers of ribbon with fine wire.

After the wedding, frame the fan in a shadow box, or place the nosegay under a glass dome as a memento of the happy occasion.

WEDDING TABLE DECORATIONS

If a reception or a party follows the wedding, plan the table decorations to match the bride's bouquet. For a fan theme, use inexpensive paper fans, spray them white and decorate with pansies, roses, lilies-of-the-valley, daisies, mock-orange blossoms or other appropriate flowers. Use small plate stands, painted white, to hold the fans and place them at angles to one another or back to back on the table. For greenery, use sprays of fresh English ivy.

Following a nosegay theme, use several to match the bride's pink one on circles of fresh English ivy at each end of the table. In the

Fig. 19

center, use three nosegays each held upright in a small glass; surround with fresh greens. Over the center of the table, use hanging nosegays. Make them according to the directions under *mobiles* (see index) using white lace doilies and adding a circle of gathered net and streamers of ribbon at the bottom of the design on both sides. Suspend five nosegays on satin ribbon of uneven lengths. The mobile effect of nosegays in slight motion will be most charming. Clear plastic balls, described on page 69, could be filled with matching flowers and used instead of the nosegays.

An even more elegant centerpiece for the table would be a large tree of fresh greens trimmed with pink nosegays. In a white urn, bend chicken wire in the shape of a tree. Insert small pieces of boxwood or cedar to completely cover. Wire a number of nosegays on the green background. Smaller trees, decorated in the same manner, may be used at each end of the table or nosegays may be placed on circles of greens.

PLACE CARDS WITH A BRIDAL THEME   Follow the bridal theme with place cards for the guests. To match the bride's fan, attach a miniature fan trimmed with tiny flowers to a folded card four-by-five inches in size. For a nosegay on a place card, gather narrow ribbon to make a circle, place three streamers under it and glue to the folded card. Fill the center with tiny florets.

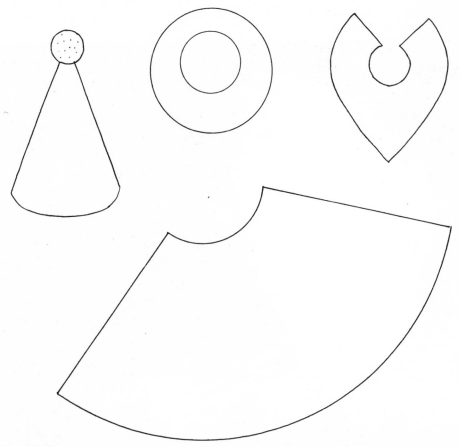

Patterns for Fig. 19

BRIDESMAIDS' LUNCHEON

Decorate the table with miniature bridesmaids marching down the table. Figure 19. Paint the cone cup and the top of the head in a pastel color. All colors are available in small quantities for a few cents at hobby stores. A cork or white styrofoam ball for the head and chenille for the arms also may be obtained from hobby stores. Using vegetable coloring, tint cotton yellow for the hair and glue in place around the head. Cut white or pastel-colored doilies for the overskirt, blouse and hat brim, and glue each piece in place. Where the hat meets the head, glue narrow ribbon, ending in streamers down the back. Use a flesh-colored paint for the face and add facial features

XXVIII.   A shower for the bride features garden flowers preserved with silica gel, and pretty parasols.

with crayons. For the nosegay, gather narrow ribbon, glue around a circle of paper and add several streamers. Fill the center with Peruvian starflowers, florets of forget-me-not and spirea and attach to the bridesmaid with glue.

BRIDAL SHOWER

To cover the gifts for a bridal shower, decorate an inexpensive paper umbrella. Plate 28. First, spray it white and glue on net tufts, roses, asters, lilies-of-the-valley, larkspurs, fern and streamers of ribbon around the top. Around the outer edge of the umbrella, tack on gathered net with needle and thread and glue on a few flowers here and there.

PLACE CARDS   For guests, make place cards from a folded four-by-five-inch card, trim with a miniature umbrella, sprayed white, and decorate with small flowers and a ribbon bow.

ANNIVERSARY DINNER

Plate 29 shows a double-ring centerpiece that can be viewed from all sides; it is most appropriate for a dinner table. Use two sizes of sewing hoops for His and Hers and cover with gold rub-on paint. Join them together, side by side, with adhesive tape. Secure them in an upright position with wire pulled through a ten-inch circle of white styrofoam, which is one inch thick. Attach pink net tufts to halves of round toothpicks with fine wire and cover the top and sides of the circle. At the base of the rings, add flowers and foliage. Perhaps you might like the centerpiece all in white. Follow the same directions, using white net tufts to cover the base. For decorating the base I suggest white roses, larkspur, bridal wreath, candytuft, hyacinths, daisies, lily-of-the-valley blooms and foliage, plus delicate fern. For a Golden Wedding Anniversary, use yellow net tufts, roses, snapdragons and tulips.

PLACE CARDS   Make a place card from a folded four-by-five-inch card, attach with glue a small plastic ring, rubbed with gold paint, and trim with three florets of blue forget-me-nots for the ring stones.

VIII   For Gifts and Bazaars

Handmade articles are becoming increasingly popular, and an open market exists for hand-crafted merchandise. Many of the ideas in this book can be used to start a money-making business or to raise funds to benefit charities, churches and other organizations. Some suggestions for suitable articles are given in this chapter. Here are a few additional ideas (see index for page numbers).

Wall panels would make an excellent do-it-yourself kit.

Butterflies can also be made from heavy cardboard. Rattan for basket-making, heavy twine or pipe cleaners can be used to outline the sections and over-all shape of the butterflies.

Seed mosiacs are very popular and can be made in many interesting designs.

Pressed flower pictures.

Small shadow boxes from ham and sardine cans.

Lamp bases with decorated shades.

Floral pictures.

Drawer pulls.

Pincushions.

Jewelry boxes.

Decorative eggs and panoramas.

Candles.

Pomanders.

DECORATED CANS AND BOTTLES

Save tin cans in all sizes to make attractive and useful containers. Decorate them with dried flowers, shells, cones or pods and use them throughout the home. Paint them in colors harmonious to their surroundings or wrap the can with twine for a rough texture and apply glue at intervals to hold rows in place. Shellac for a natural finish or color with paint. Keep a few painted cans on hand to quickly decorate for a gift. Treasure Jewel rub-on paints (see Sources of Supply) will transform a simple can into an object of beauty. Tall coffee cans make good kitchen canisters. Paint them as described and paste a collage of coffee beans on the canister for coffee, rice for the rice canister, and an assortment of whole spices to identify the contents. One I like, particularly for the shut-in, is a low tuna can decorated with a few flowers and foliage and filled with small note cards. Sometimes you can find note cards imprinted with the same flowers you have used on the can.

TWINE HOLDERS   Empty peanut cans make a useful twine holder. Punch a hole in the lid with an ice pick to string the cord through. Place a loop of adhesive tape on one side to hold a small pair of scissors. Paint the can and decorate with cones, pods and sea shells.

Plastic detergent bottles also make attractive twine holders. Figure 20. Create a birdhouse by cutting a round bottle on a slant to the height of about five inches. Make a round hole in the front for the twine. Using glue, cover the top with a square of heavy cardboard for the roof, allowing a small overhang. Attach another piece of cardboard to the bottom for the platform. Spray-paint the birdhouse and decorate with flowers, cones, pods or sea shells. Perch a little bird on a twig across the front for added interest.

GIFTS WITH FRAGRANCE

SACHET   Something different in the way of a sachet is a decorated tea strainer. Figure 21. The strainers are available in a large size for the teapot and a smaller size for a cup. Cover the strainers with gold rub-on paint or Treasure Jewel in a pastel color. (See Sources of Supply.) Decorate the top with tiny pine cones, Peruvian star flowers, bits of celosia and a bow of ribbon. Sprinkle sachet powder on a ball of cotton and place inside the strainer. Hang them in a closet for a touch of fragrance.

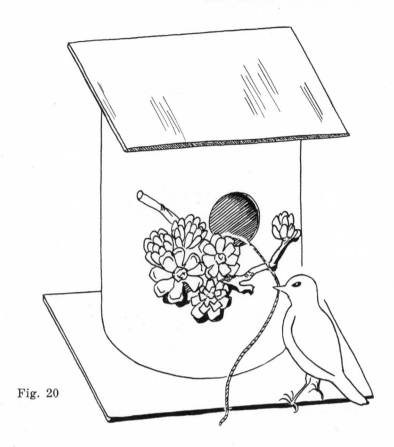

Fig. 20

FRAGRANCE JARS   Another gift item, so very easy to make, is a fragrance jar. This will require only rose petals, herbs and spices. Petals from full-blown roses about ready to shed are the ones to use. To dry the petals, cover the bottom of container with silica gel and then spread the petals so they are not touching, slowly sprinkle silica gel until each petal is covered. Add another layer of petals and continue the process until the container is full. After three days, remove from the silica gel and they are ready for the jar.

Select a decorative, clear glass jar for the colorful rose petals. For a pint-sized container, add two whole cloves and two mace, a very small piece of ginger bark and a few dried leaves of rosemary, lavender and lemon thyme. On the top layer of your petals, place several small rosebuds. Close the jar tightly for several weeks. For a finishing touch attach a pretty bow to the neck of the jar. The fragrance jar is especially appropriate for the bedroom or powder room. Before a

Fig. 21

guest arrives, remove the lid for an hour or so to release a delightful aroma in the room. (To preserve, keep jar covered at other times.)

BUTTERFLIES

Just the gift for the person who has everything! Decorate plastic butterflies to be attached to window curtains or used in flower arrangements. These butterflies come in soft pastels and cost about ten cents each. Using a yellow butterfly, cover the body with bits of pink celosia —it will look like velvet. Spot the wings with florets of blue forget-me-not. Spray the finished butterfly with Seymour's Clear Plastic Spray #11-821 to prevent color-fading by the sun.

LIQUID PLASTIC

This craft has opened a new and exciting field for the use of dried materials. Colorful dried materials are a prerequisite for casting in clear plastic. Make a very special gift for the bride and groom—one they will cherish for life! Dry a sprig of lily-of-the-valley from the bride's bouquet and embed it in the handle of a cake server. The mold for the handle is available at hobby stores. Purchase a cake server with a wooden handle and replace it with the one you make. The directions with the liquid plastic explain how to attach the handle. I suggest that you color the last layer of plastic green and this will be the background for the flower. A tray, paperweight or coasters would be appropriate for some of the flowers from the bride's bouquet. Preserving and making these sentimental items can be quite a paying hobby.

Glass caster cups make an excellent mold for a paperweight. Embed a flower, shells, tiny pine cones or bits of broken glass for the decorative motif. Use all-purpose plastic resin (the rigid type—see Sources of Supply.) I shall not tell you how to use liquid plastic because complete instructions are included with the material.

ACCESSORIES FOR A DESK

Accessories for the desk, suitably decorated, make attractive and unusual gifts. Plate 30. A magnifying paperweight of flowers is cherished by a person of any age. You will find these paperweights in ten-cent and stationery stores. Remove the felt from the bottom, and you will have a hollow space for dried materials. Cut a piece of heavy paper in an appropriate color the size of the bottom. To this, glue small florets, miniature flowers and fern; allow to dry overnight. Glue circle with the design to the bottom of paperweight and cover with green felt. This is an intriguing accessory for a man's desk in shades of red, orange, yellow and brown—using tiny yellow roses and Peruvian starflowers, bits of orange celosia, small buds of dusty miller and brown dock. For a feminine touch, use miniature roses, violas, florets of forget-me-not, bridal wreath and delicate green fern.

For other desk accessories, glue a few flowers, cones or shells to the top of a stamp box. (Unfinished boxes may be obtained from any hobby store.) Attach a group of dried flowers to a straw letter basket. To fasten, use wire stems on flowers and foliage and push the wire through the straw to the inside and twist. Plain, inexpensive, metal book ends, purchased from ten-cent or book stores, can be painted and decorated with dried materials, adding charm to any room.

PINE CONES THAT BURN WITH VARI-COLORED FLAMES

Coat pine cones with liquid wax (some inexpensive brand). Mix equal quantities of the following chemicals in a large salt shaker and sprinkle over the pine cones while the wax is still damp. Let dry and package for gifts or pile in a basket by your own fireplace.

These chemicals make the variety of colors:

Cupric Sulfate green
Calcium Chloride orange
Potassium Chloride violet
Sodium Chloride yellow
Lithium Sulfate red

All chemicals may be purchased from drug stores or chemical supply companies. (See Sources of Supply.)

Many of these items made with inexpensive materials are easy for children to make for gifts and money-making school projects.

XXX.   You can make novel gifts using dried flowers, seeds, pine cones and other natural materials. These decorative desk accessories will last indefinitely.

GREETING CARDS

Attractive greeting cards with a personal message are meaningful and fun to make (Color Plate IV), and of course your handiwork will be cherished by the recipient. One friend still displays on her desk a dried-flower card sent several Christmases ago. What better way can one find to wish a speedy recovery to a sick friend? Or to say "hello" to a relative far away? From a stationer or printer, obtain heavy paper in pastels. Cut and fold paper to the size desired. (Match it to the box or envelope in which it will be mailed.) The card can be trimmed with gold matting of the type used for découpage (Gold-Dec-it—see Sources of Supply). A bit of lace and velvet can be glued to the card as a back-

ground for the flowers. First, outline your design with bits of green fern or cedar, gluing each item in place. Use a larger flower in the center as a focal point, work out with progressively smaller blooms and finish the edges with tiny buds and florets. The photograph illustrates miniature roses, zinnias, tiny Johnny-jump-ups, florets of lilac, forget-me-not, hydrangea, bridal wreath, small pieces of pink celosia and dusty miller. A small, thin box should be used for mailing so flowers will not crush. Or, use a heavy envelope but make your design of flat pressed flowers.

Why not make personal Christmas cards? Use plain note cards and, in the upper corner, glue a miniature red rosebud with green cedar; or cut red celosia in the shape of petals and form a flower; or cut red nandina berries in half and group three together with small leaves as a sprig of holly. (Spray berries with Seymour's Clear Plastic Spray #11-821 to preserve their redness.)

There is a kit now available for making decorative greeting cards. (See Sources of Supply.) The kit contains only white material for the cards and rice paper which is used to cover the dried materials. However, you can buy heavy cardpaper in varied colors from printer or hobby stores. Many printers have cuttings from large sheets which they will give you. In this procedure of cardmaking, you must use flat pressed flowers and foliage. On page 28 you will find directions for pressing materials. Color Plate IV illustrates pieces of 'Silver King' (dusty miller), yellow petals to form a daisy and petals of blue cornflowers. Hold the materials in place with a touch of glue and cover the card with a piece of rice paper from the kit. (You may substitute a single thickness of facial tissue.) Thin Elmer's or Sobo adhesive to one-third glue and two-thirds water, and using a soft, stubby brush, carefully cover the tissue with the solution. When it dries, the flowers will have a frosty appearance. Make some small thank-you cards using just petals of cornflowers as shown in the photograph. You can create many original and artistic card designs at practically no cost.

WRAPPINGS

A personalized gift wrapping is sheer delight for the recipient! It adds an affectionate postscript even to the smallest and most inexpensive package. Imaginative ways with wrappings increase the fun of giving. Ribbons and dried flowers help you create a variety of distinctive designs.

In Color Plate XI, the design of the stocking hints at its contents. The paper is pink and the design is cut from black lace. First draw the stocking on a piece of tissue paper, place the paper on the lace and machine-stitch around the edge. This stitching will give a more distinct outline for the design. Tear off the paper, trim close to the stitching and glue onto the package. The garter of pleated pink satin ribbon is trimmed with miniature red roses and baby's-breath. The box is finished with ribbon around the edge, ending with a looped bow on top.

Any young miss will be "pleased pink" with her gift of gloves. Cut the glove from pink felt and trim with rose buds, lilies-of-the-valley, florets of blue hydrangea and fern.

For grandmother's gift, use pale blue paper and a four-inch silver doily and top with a circle of gathered blue net. Fill the center with small purple pansies and lavender scillas. Add several streamers of purple velvet ribbon to complete the nosegay design.

A topiary tree of green cedar and halves of red nandina berries on moss green paper has the out-of-doors touch and would be appropriate for any male. The trunk and pot are cut from velvet-textured green ribbon and all materials are attached with glue. This design in miniature is stunning on a greeting card or in an enlarged version would focus Christmas greetings on any door.

You need only a few flowers to add a special touch to any gift package. Old-fashioned roses on the small package convey a message of love.

IX   Dried Flower Arrangements

Dried flowers offer the beginner a real opportunity to learn how to make flower arrangements. You can practice as much as you like, stop any time, and pick up again when convenient, never fearing that the flowers will wilt. This you cannot do with fresh flowers.

Since a flower arrangement is an art form, it should be used as a method of self-expression, with the ultimate goal always the same: that you make it a creative, expressive and enjoyable experience. My motto is "relax, don't hurry, have fun."

Dried arrangements can be changed often. Enjoy a mass design for a month or two, then take some of the flowers and make a line design. By keeping a supply of dried flowers and foliage on hand, an arrangement can be available on short notice. When guests arrive unexpectedly, or you decide to have a last-minute party, it's just a step to your closet to find the makings for a floral decoration.

Once you have mastered the basic principles, you can say that there are five steps in making any arrangement: deciding on its location, choosing the flowers, selecting the container, grouping flowers for color harmony and unity, and executing the design.

THE BASIC ART PRINCIPLES

To achieve a good design, certain art principles must be understood and applied. Let's discuss them separately with the comment that they are all mutually dependent.

BALANCE   Every design must have stability, actual and visual. Balance can be symmetrical or asymmetrical. In symmetrical balance, an imaginary vertical axis divides the arrangement into two halves, more or less equal. That is, plant material similar or identical in color and weight is used on both sides of the imagined center. Color Plate VI is an example of balance by symmetry. In asymmetrical balance, the plant materials on each side of the axis are not identical, and the axis is usually *off* center. Balance can be achieved by correct evaluation and use of design elements. For example, dark intense colors and heavy textures weigh more than light colors and smooth surfaces. Balance can also be achieved by placement. This may be explained in terms of a seesaw. The lighter the child, the further out on a seesaw he must sit for balance; the heavier, the closer to the axis. Similarly, larger flowers and leaves and more intense colors should be placed nearer the axis to create a feeling of balance.

THE AREA OR CENTER OF INTEREST   This plays an important part in the balance of an arrangement. It is usually the point in a design towards which the lines seem to converge and, in traditional flower arrangement, occurs at the opening in the container from which all stems radiate.

RHYTHM   It is characterized by the repetition of design elements in a pattern of flow and movement. There is a recurrence of lines, of line directions, of colors, sizes, shapes and textures. For example, to achieve a sense of recurrence or rhythm in color, use the darkest color value at the center of interest in your arrangement and gradually fill in with medium colors until at the outer edges you place the lightest, palest hues. Use the same treatment for shapes and forms: large forms at the center of interest, gradually leading to smallest and least textured ones at the periphery.

CONTRAST   Again, all the elements of the design may be set off against one another to create difference which is the essence of design. The differences may be striking, as with black and white, horizontal and vertical, smooth and rough, or they may be subtle as with pale grey and white, etc. If the contrast is subtle, the effect is usually delicate and formal; with sharp contrast, the effect is dramatic.

In midwinter, shapeless snow and endless shadows make us long for brilliant color and strong contrasts of form. So all through the summer, dry materials for variety of color, size, shape and texture.

Then on a dismal day, your house can come alive with a rich tapestry made from plants preserved as much for their differences as for their similarities.

DOMINANCE   This art principle refers to the authority or control which one element of design must exert over another, and of course it immediately implies that difference must exist. (There can be no dominance when two units are identical.) In practice, this means that you select and use hues, sizes, shapes, lines, directions, etc., so that one aspect or combination becomes pre-eminent. A brilliant flower, an unusual texture, a bold leaf—this powerful element should exert dominant influence.

SCALE AND PROPORTION   These refer to the size relationship of parts of the design to themselves, and to the whole. The so-called rule that an arrangement must be at least one and one-half times the height of the container, or one and one-half times the width of a low container, is flexible. If the tallest material is light and feathery, you may increase up to three times the height of the container. The space the arrangement occupies will determine these proportions.

THE ELEMENTS OF DESIGN

Lines, colors, textures, patterns and forms are the ingredients of design. As all of the flowers are stripped of their leaves before they are dried, basic ingredients are reduced to a minimum, which simplifies your task. You can select flowers for their own shape, adding whatever leaves you deem necessary to get precisely the effect you want.

LINE   The need to wire the stems of dried flowers can be a blessing, since your design can take on the line direction you wish it to, rather than following nature. However, be sure to manipulate the wire so that the stems seem natural and graceful, not stiff and angular.

COLOR   There are practically no clashing colors in dried flowers. The reason is that as the flowers become ever so slightly quieter in tone, they become more neutral and therefore blend better. However, this quieting is not fading. As you will see in the color illustrations, flowers dried in silica gel need not lose their effective coloring, the change in many plants being so slight as to be imperceptible. (Chapter II lists some colors and plants which *do* change color.)

The color of the foliage you use should be carefully considered. If the flowers have dried in subtle tones, I prefer leafage of rather muted grey-green. Fresh or dried artemisia, lavender and rosemary are good choices, rather than strong green leaves which would over-power the subtle color. Blue-green foliage is fine with flowers dried in pink, purple and blue tones. Bronzy foliage and the yellow-green leaves of English laurel go well with the bright yellows and oranges of marigolds and zinnias, for example, which do not lose any apparent color. The vivid green leaves of the butterfly bush are good with bright colors.

TEXTURE   Since texture is an important ingredient of design, foliage which has a great deal of surface interest should be included in your supply of dried materials. Leaves with a strong silhouette through which light and dark penetrate, as ferns and peonies, offer exciting patterns too. In this category are velvety textured lamb's-ears (*Stachys lanata*), satiny lily-of-the-valley, variegated heartleaf (*Asarum virginicum*) and many others.

PATTERN   The pattern of an arrangement is determined by how you place the solids of plants and other materials, and by the voids or spaces which result. Good designers give as much thought to designing the space as the solids.

FORM   The shape or outline of your arrangement can be based on the familiar crescent, circle, triangle, Hogarth or S curve, or any segment thereof. Or you can be modern and follow the parabola, or even the free-form shapes which biologists discovered under their microscopes. Just be sure you have some shape in mind when you make your arrangement.

THE MECHANICS

Since preserved flowers do not require water, you are free to use almost any type of vase or holder. With stems of wire, it is possible for you to insert flowers and foliage at the exact place and angle which best fulfills your design concept. Here are three suggestions for me-chanical aids:

Affix a pinholder to the bottom of the container with Tacky Tape. (See Sources of Supply.)

Press dry Oasis firmly onto the pins. You can easily stick filler

materials, wire stems, wooden sticks, etc., into the Oasis, and remove them just as easily. Do not use Styrofoam; it is much too
hard for brittle stems.

To combine freshly cut foliage or flowers with dried ones, soak
a block of Oasis in water until thoroughly wet. Drain, place in
the container, and completely outline the design with the fresh
materials. Add wire to the dried flowers in the lengths needed
and insert them in the arrangement for color harmony. Combine
roses with clipped pine; marigolds or zinnias with English laurel;
hardy begonias and baby's breath with dainty fern.

FOR A TALL CONTAINER   Cut Oasis a little larger than the opening.
Wedge dry Oasis firmly into place, letting it extend an inch or two
above the rim. This permits you to insert flowers and foliage at any
angle.

CONTAINERS

There is a wider choice of containers for dried flowers than for fresh
ones. The metal container whose seams are not watertight, a shallow
piece of driftwood, the pottery pitcher with a crack in the bottom—
all of these can be made to function as vases, provided their color is
right. An inexpensive container in a neutral tone—gray, off white
or quiet green, for example—can be far more pleasing than a costly
vase ornamented with painted flowers, if the painted ones are more
brilliant than dried ones. Old copper, pewter and silver, with their
lovely patina, can be effective foils for dried material. Straw baskets,
weathered wood, primitive earthy-toned pottery, are usually harmonious in color quality. However, the containers need not be colorless.
One of my favorites is a Bristol blue stem glass which I use in contrast
with pink to red flowers. If there is a rule to follow it is this: don't
let the container overpower the plant material in color or size.

*XXXI.   (Opposite)   Driftwood establishes the curvilinear design for this
arrangement of chrysanthemums, green ligustrum berries and nandina
foliage.*

THE SETTING

One of the most important steps in connection with the arrangement, is deciding where it will be placed. Flowers have tremendous attention-getting quality and create an immediate aura of graciousness in a room. In fact, it is difficult to imagine a truly lovely home without them. Because they are so important, flowers should be arranged and designed with their setting in mind. Only after you have determined this do you have a concrete basis for selecting the flowers, container, and the form and pattern of the composition.

The whole task is made easier if you have an abundant stock of dried flowers in varied colors, for then you are free to make selections according to your decorating needs, without first wondering whether the garden is cooperating by producing the blossoms you need. Of course, marvelous as silica gel is, it won't transform color discords into harmonies, or change tiny blooms into important big ones. Having the right flowers for drying depends on your planting the right seeds or seedlings, so plant your garden with some thought for your decorating needs.

TYPES OF FLOWER ARRANGEMENTS

Contemporary American arrangements generally are classified as line, mass or mass-line designs.

LINE DESIGN   A line arrangement uses little material. Characteristically, it has a dominant line direction, and an open silhouette. A piece of driftwood or a dried, bare branch from the woods can create a dramatic linear quality. Plate 31. Wisteria and wild honeysuckle are useful. The leaves of honeysuckle dry to a velvety texture and retain their original color.

Figurines combined with a few flowers make an unusual line arrangement. In Plate 32, a figure of St. Francis in a light clay color is combined with dried Peace roses and lupine foliage. A small piece of dry Oasis on a pinpoint holder at the base of the figurine secures

XXXII.   (Opposite)   Beautifully dried "Peace" roses complement the figurine of St. Francis and the birds.

Fig. 22

the arrangement. Shiny, washed rocks in shades of soft brown add a touch of nature to cover the mechanics.

MASSED DESIGN   Gay and colorful, a massed design has depth and fullness. The essentials are that it have a closed silhouette and more solids than voids. Quantities of materials are grouped by kinds and colors so that they give a sense of form *within* the mass. The outline or shape of this type of arrangement may be oval, fan-shaped or triangular.

MASSED LINE DESIGN   This combines line and mass and is three-dimensional. Color Plate VI shows an arrangement predominantly line with light mass added only for depth.

MAKING A MASS ARRANGEMENT

Color Plate IX shows a massed design in a goblet. The procedure for making this type is shown in Figure 22. Firmly wedge a piece of Oasis in the container. Let the Oasis extend at least an inch or two above the rim of the container to allow the insertion of flowers and foliage at any angle. First, establish the highest point of your design with dusty miller, grasses or other airy material. This height should be at least one and one-half to two times the height of the container. Continue to outline the design with the same light, airy material and then fill in the voids with materials such as larkspur, statice, delphinium, rosebuds, sprigs of white spirea, blue salvia and tiny straw-flowers. By placing materials alternately on each side and working down from the top, you will keep your arrangement in balance. Tuck in pieces of green hydrangea, fern, lily-of-the-valley leaves (use reverse side of leaf for satin texture), and lovely velvet-textured lamb's ears (*Stachys lanata*). You will now have a compact background for the final flowers. Establish your area of interest low at the rim of the container, allowing a flower or leaf to extend over the edge. Here group your brightest and darkest colors and large forms of flowers. They weigh more, hence should be used at the center of interest for the sake of balance. Just above and to each side of the focal point, use a gradual change in size and color of flowers, making them blend into the established background. Add vivid blue hydrangea and touches of white (daisies, pansies or candytuft) for accent.

The arrangement shown in Color Plate VIII includes roses, hydrangeas, snapdragons, carnations, larkspurs, asters, forget-me-nots, daisies, ferns, grasses and dusty miller. The dome, sixteen inches high, is on a twelve-inch base. In the middle of the wooden base, secure a two-inch pinpoint holder with florist's clay. Figure 23. Cut a piece of dry Oasis three by seven inches, and push firmly down on the pinpoints. This allows you to use short stemmed flowers from top to bottom. Starting at the bottom, insert foliage and flowers at about a 45° angle to cover mechanics. Place a piece of fern or dusty miller at the top to establish the height of dome. Then cover the entire Oasis with small pieces of green hydrangea to give a compact background. Insert flowers and foliage staying within the circle of the base so that the flowers will not touch the edge of dome. Not only does the dome protect your arrangement, but the glass reflects the beautiful colors of the flowers. Since this type of arrangement may be viewed from all sides, it would be good as a centerpiece; it is charming with antiques or distinctive in a modern setting.

With a few flowers in bold colors or combined with a figurine, you can make a contemporary line arrangement to display under the dome. At Christmas, lift the pinpoint containing the arrangement, store it away in a plastic bag and use your dome for a design of holiday trimmings. These domes may be obtained in all sizes, appropriate for many places throughout the home. (See Sources of Supply.) Treat yourself to a large one and enjoy it for a lifetime.

MODERN DESIGN

The modern flower arrangement promotes self-expression, giving the arranger freedom to expand and interpret her ideas and emotions. It usually is linear. Plate 33 shows a modern arrangement with weathered wood sprayed black. It is an interpretation of the darkness of night turning to the light of day with the rising sun. Bright yellow marigolds, glued to a styrofoam ball and mounted on metal tubing, represent the sun. The curvature of the driftwood traces the path of the sun rising.

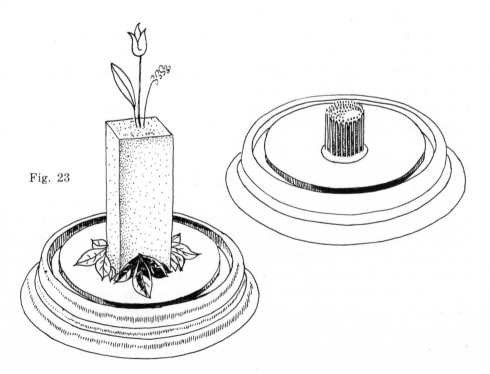

Fig. 23

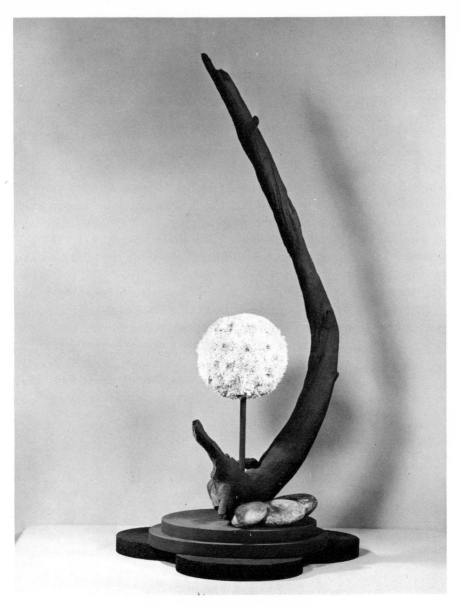

XXXIII.   SUN—"*That orbed continent, the fire that severs day from night . . ."—Shakespeare. An interpretative design.*

PRESERVING YOUR DRIED ARRANGEMENTS

Humidity must be considered in caring for dried flowers. Some flowers are very susceptible to atmospheric conditions because their porous nature still exists after drying. It is best not to use dried flowers in humid summer weather unless your rooms are air-conditioned. Some flowers, however, are not affected by humidity and will last for years. Their durability, of course, depends on the substance and texture of the flower itself. Dried flowers naturally keep better in winter when the rooms are heated. As mentioned earlier, several light sprayings of transparent lacquer (Seymour's Clear Plastic Spray #11-821) will preserve the flowers and a periodic light spraying will freshen and restore the color.

Filler materials such as dusty miller, salvia, baby's-breath and grasses can be used many times. They make the skeleton or shape of your arrangement. Simply by replacing the faded flowers with new, colorful ones, and adding green foliage, your arrangement is ready to use again.

I suggest that you read good books on flower arranging, visit flower shows and keep an open mind to develop your ideas.

X Antiqued Flowers

A new and popular hobby is antiquing flowers, foliage and fruit. A simple treatment can transform the materials into objects of rich beauty.

I enjoy the colors of freshly dried flowers and make new arrangements each fall. However, I often take last year's arrangement and spray it gold; the various forms and textures make an interesting design and the arrangement will last for years. To brighten, spray each year. Color Plate X.

To antique colorful dried flowers and green foliage, give the materials three light sprayings of Pearly Dew (see Sources of Supply) for a "pearlized" effect. Using a small artist's brush, lightly apply gold rub-on paint, thinned with turpentine, to the tips of flower petals and foliage. Because of the brittleness of dried materials, arrange with dry Oasis in the container as explained in Chapter IX.

PLASTIC

Inexpensive plastic (polyethylene) flowers from the dime store also can be antiqued with a very simple treatment. Mix together one pint of turpentine and one-half pint of light oak varnish. To this, add three ounces of gold paint. A two-pound coffee tin makes a good container for the mixture. Cut the individual flowers and foliage from the main plastic stem, leaving about an inch of individual stem. Stir the mixture to bring the gold paint to the surface and slowly dip each flower head and piece of foliage in the mixture. Shake off the excess liquid by hitting the sides of the can. Attach a small piece of freezer tape to the end of the stem and bend it over the bar of a wire coat hanger. Place the hangers on a clothes line, using newspaper beneath to catch any dripping. Let the materials dry overnight. (Note: Since small amounts of gold paint cling to the materials in the dipping process, more gold must be added to the mixture from time to time if you are dipping quantities of material.)

For added color with a satin luster, rub on Treasure Jewel (see Sources of Supply) in appropriate colors. Artificial fruit, rubbed with this type of paint, is beautiful.

To arrange the antiqued plastic flowers, secure a piece of green styrofoam in the container with Tacky Tape. Attach a round tooth-pick to the short stems of flowers and foliage with freezer tape and proceed to make your design. Styrofoam is suggested for plastic flowers on wooden picks because these flowers are not brittle like dried ones.

Antiqued flowers with stems removed can be glued to any surface for a decorative note. Make a design in a shadow box with an antique frame; decorate the tops of novelty boxes; trim dresser and desk accessories; encircle an antique mirror.

Inexpensive and attractive containers for antiqued flowers are clay flower pots colored with rub-on paints. Also available are Gold'n Color spray paints (see Sources of Supply), in such combinations as gold-red, silver-blue, gold-grape, gold-green and many more.

Sources of Supply

FLOWER-DRI AND FLOWER-DRI KIT
Plantabbs Corporation, Lutherville-Timonium, Md. 21093

LIQUID PLASTIC, PLASTIC RESIN
Hazel Pearson Handicrafts, P.O. Box 193, Temple City, Calif. 91781
Suggested booklets: Casting in Clear Plastic; Liquid Plastic Artistry

PANORAMA
Lee Ward, Elgin, Illinois 60121

GOLD-DEC-IT, PLASTIC BALLS
Dorothy Harrower, River Road, Upper Black Eddy, Buck County, Pa.

GREETING CARD KIT
Takashimaya, Inc., 562 Fifth Avenue, New York 36, N.Y.

GLASS DOMES
Downs and Company, 1014 Davis Street, Evanston, Illinois

TACKY TAPE
Schnee Moreland Chemical Corp., Box 1305, Irving, Texas

TREASURE JEWEL, TREASURE GOLD
Connoisseur Studio, Inc., P.O. Box 7187, Louisville, Ky.

GOLD RUB & BUFF, PEARLY DEW, GOLD'N COLORS
Cavalier Handicrafts, 1839 West Broad Street, Richmond, Virginia

FLOWER-DRI	CALCIUM CHLORIDE
ORRIS ROOT	POTASSIUM CHLORIDE
SANDALWOOD	SODIUM CHLORIDE
CUPRIC SULFATE	LITHIUM SULFATE

Cardinal Products, P.O. Box 1611, Durham, North Carolina

SUPPLIES FOR FLOWER ARRANGERS
Dorothy Biddle Service, 8 Broadway, Hawthorne, New York
Floral Art, P. O. Box 394, Highland Station, Springfield, Mass.
Garden Club Products, 591 Hillside Avenue, Needham Heights, Mass.

INDEX